ACTIVITIES
LINKING
SCIENCE
WITH
MATH
K-4

ACTIVITIES
LINKING
SCIENCE
WITH
MATH
K-4

John Eichinger

NSTApress

National Science Teachers Association

Arlington, Virginia

National Science Teachers Association

Claire Reinburg, Director
Jennifer Horak, Managing Editor
Judy Cusick, Senior Editor
Andrew Cocke, Associate Editor

ART AND DESIGN
Will Thomas Jr., Director
Joseph Butera, Graphic Designer, cover and interior design

PRINTING AND PRODUCTION
Catherine Lorrain, Director

NATIONAL SCIENCE TEACHERS ASSOCIATION
Francis Q. Eberle, PhD, Executive Director
David Beacom, Publisher

LIBRARY OF CONGRESS CATALOGING-IN-PUBLICATION DATA
Eichinger, John.
  Activities linking science with mathematics, grades K–4 / by John Eichinger.
      p. cm.
  Includes bibliographical references and index.
  ISBN 978-1-933531-42-7
  1. Science--Study and teaching (Elementary)--Activity programs. 2. Mathematics--Study and
teaching (Elementary)--Activity programs. 3. Interdisciplinary approach in education. I. Title.
  LB1585.E36 2009
  372.3'5044--dc22
                            2009003257

+ Table of Contents

Earth Science

Life Science

Acknowledgments

I would like to thank NSTA Press for supporting this probe into integrated science instruction and am particularly indebted to Claire Reinburg and Jennifer Horak for their clear vision and expert guidance. I am grateful to the reviewers for sharing their excellent comments and insights, and offer special thanks to my education students at California State University, Los Angeles, who continue to enlighten and inspire me. Thanks also to my colleagues Chogollah Maroufi, Paul Narguizian, and Gregory Toliver for their generous encouragement and feedback. I am especially grateful to my wife, Danube, and my sons, Wolfe and Björn, for their unwavering patience and boundless support, without which this book would not exist.

John Eichinger

Lovingly dedicated to Danube, Wolfe, and Björn

+ Introduction

"The solution which I am urging, is to eradicate the fatal disconnection of subjects which kills the vitality of our modern curriculum. There is only one subject matter for education, and that is Life in all its manifestations."

Alfred North Whitehead
(The Aims of Education 1929)

Overview

Activities Linking Science With Mathematics, Grades K–4 (ALSM) rejects traditional, discipline-bound methods of instruction and instead opens the door to hands-on, discovery-based, and academically rigorous activities that link various scientific disciplines to mathematics in particular, but also to visual arts, social sciences, and language arts. These 20 activities, intended for inservice and preservice K–4 teachers, align with the National Science Education Standards (NSES) and the National Council of Teachers of Mathematics (NCTM) standards, both of which encourage an increase in interdisciplinary instruction. The lessons balance integrated content with the processes of personally relevant inquiry and are designed to promote creative, critical thinking on the part of all students. The lessons are also teacher friendly, requiring no advanced expertise in any particular subject area and using inexpensive and easy-to-find materials.

ALSM is an engaging supplement to core classroom curriculum that allows all teachers to maintain high expectations with effective, authentic, and student-centered instruction. Preservice teachers in particular benefit from the early introduction to these sorts of strategies, helping them develop effective interdisciplinary classroom instruction. Indeed, as McComas and Wang noted, teachers must "experience effective blended science instruction models firsthand" for true interdisciplanry models ever to flourish in our education system (1998, p. 345). To that end, *ALSM* models alternative, yet proven, teaching practices that can be applied in any classroom. The activities are particularly well suited to urban schools, where access

to natural study sites such as lakes, streams, and forest trails, or even small plots of grass are limited. What's more, the focus on individual student observations and cooperative group work (rather than teacher-centered lectures, traditional textbooks, or pencil-and-paper tests) as the basis for conceptual understanding levels the playing field among students of different genders, cultures, and native languages.

As you acquaint yourself with the *ALSM* approach, keep in mind that though classroom ready, these 20 activities are intended to be neither rigid nor overly prescriptive. Think of them as models, jumping off points, and let the active, constructivist approach to teaching inspire you to develop and implement your own academically integrated lessons that stimulate the natural curiosity and problem-solving skills of your students.

Theoretical Foundation

Educational constructivists believe meaningful learning depends on prior experience (Piaget 1970). Understanding is mediated by personal and social background; knowledge is constructed, negotiated, and tested via experience. The only adequate test of knowledge, then, is its viability when applied to current problems (Tobin 1993). Constructivism does not outline a particular methodology but generally suggests that you consider students' prior experience (and even misconceptions), create situations in which students have opportunities to reconceptualize naive ideas, and remain flexible and alert to the growth and viability of student knowledge. As von Glasersfeld noted, "successful thinking is more important than 'correct' answers," and to foster motivation, the constructivist teacher will "create situations where the students have an opportunity to experience the pleasure inherent in solving a problem" (1993, p. 33). *ALSM* combines this attention to students' experience and successful thinking with classroom lessons and pedagogic strategies you'll quickly recognize: hands-on and minds-on instruction, guided discovery, experimentation, the learning cycle, open-ended challenges, projects, metacognition, attention to the affective domain, and authentic assessment. (A matrix clarifying the various instructional strategies used in each of the activities appears on page 12.) The activities described in the following pages push you to apply these well-known teaching techniques in novel, more student-centered ways.

Four overarching principles—each clearly recognized and encouraged by the national standards in science and mathematics—guide *ALSM* lessons (AAAS 1989, 1993; NCTM 2000, 2006; NRC 1996).

1. *Student relevance* refers to a focus on student interests, prior knowledge, questions, and ideas, as well as student-initiated projects and

solutions. In short, lessons should reflect the lives of the students involved. In the words of the National Science Education Standards: "Teachers[should] plan to meet the particular interests, knowledge, and skills of their students and build on their questions and ideas" (NRC 1996, p. 31). Relying only on teacher-directed memorization of facts is insufficient and ineffective according to a number of influential sources, including the national standards in science and mathematics (AAAS 1989, 1993; NCTM 2000; NRC 1996). If a deeper and more viable understanding is to be reached, you must help students bridge the familiar with the unfamiliar. That is, meaningful teaching begins with what students already know and connects, through active learning methods, to new, expansive concepts and understandings. *Principles and Standards for School Mathematics* states, "Mathematics makes more sense and is easier to remember and to apply when students connect new knowledge to existing knowledge in meaningful ways" (NCTM 2000, p. 20).

2. *Interaction/collaboration* reflects the fact that elementary students are fundamentally concrete thinkers who require personal and interpersonal experiences to learn effectively (Vygotsky 1978). As the National Science Education Standards explain, "Interactions among individuals and groups in the classroom can be vital in deepening the understanding of scientific concepts and the nature of scientific endeavors" (NRC 1996, p. 32). You should, therefore, actively involve students both personally and socially in science-math explorations. Engaging lessons that encourage involvement and provide opportunities for meaningful understanding are optimally motivating for students, especially in grades K–4. We also know that to be fully effective, interactive studies must be undertaken in a collaborative manner. Learning depends on socialization, and a deep understanding of science and math depends on an awareness of the interpersonal aspects of those disciplines (Vygotsky 1978). Keep in mind that well-managed group work in the classroom closely resembles the collaborative nature of real-world science, mathematics, and technology—thus offering students authentic, interactive experiences, (AAAS 1989; NRC 1996).

3. *Problem-based learning* provides a challenging and motivating context for classroom math and science exploration. An essential feature of the current national standards in math and science education is a call for deeper, more active, and more relevant inquiry. "Well-chosen tasks can pique students' curiosity and draw them into mathematics," says the

National Council of Teachers of Mathematics (NCTM 2000, p. 18). Posing realistic, interesting, open-ended, and challenging problems for students to solve is a mainstay of the reform movement. In particular, Meier, Hovde, and Meier (1996) stress the importance of realistic and interdisciplinary applications of problem solving. Through problem solving in the classroom, students learn to effectively confront real-life demands by applying higher-order thinking skills. Thus, the development of problem-solving skills through active, engaging investigation is fundamental to the national standards in science and mathematics (NCTM 2000; NRC 1996).

4. *Integrated instruction* is the blending of two or more academic disciplines into a particular classroom lesson. Science and mathematics, though traditionally treated in academia as discrete intellectual entities, are not separated in the real world. Integrated instruction not only promotes the presentation of the subjects in a realistic and relevant context but also provides opportunities for imaginative and personal connections between students and subject matter, further enhancing understanding and motivation. Cross-disciplinary connections deepen understanding by allowing students to simultaneously use the language, concepts, and methods of thinking of several subject areas. That is, students have an opportunity to view and comprehend a situation from more than one disciplinary perspective, generating a greater complexity of meaning (Fosnot 1996). Research into the impact of integrated science-math instruction shows a positive effect on student achievement, problem-solving ability, self-worth, motivation, and interest (Meier, Cobbs, and Nicol 1998). Finally, on a practical level, integrated instruction, by connecting subjects and thereby condensing teaching time, provides more time to teach science and math in what has become a very tight daily teaching schedule.

Integrated, unified, blended, interdisciplinary, cross-disciplinary, multidisciplinary, thematic, and *coordinated*—all are words used to describe simultaneous instruction in multiple disciplines. However, because these terms tend to be used inconsistently, there is a great deal of confusion about what they actually mean. Lederman and Neiss (1998) observe that *integration*, for example, tends to be used in one of two ways: First, it may refer to instructional situations where traditional boundaries are blurred or even lost. Or, it may refer to situations that maintain traditional boundaries but stress the interactions among the disciplines during instruction. Lederman and Neiss favor the second definition, explaining that conventions differ between science

and mathematics, largely due to the notion that science (and not math) must consider external empirical observations in problem-solving situations. Ways of knowing vary significantly between science and mathematics (as well as between other academic disciplines), enabling us to discriminate one discipline from another. Therefore, if students are to gain understanding of how science, math, or any other intellectual discipline functions, the lines separating the disciplines should not be erased or even significantly blurred. Rather than dissolving disciplines into incongruous hybrids, Lederman and Neiss argue that if you are interested in integrated instruction, you should help students find meaningful interconnections among existing disciplines. Although a certain amount of disciplinary "cloudiness" is bound to exist in any attempt at integrated instruction, the science-math links described in the following activities reflect the position of Lederman and Neiss.

How to Use This Book

Think of *ALSM* not as an activity book but as an instructional framework and a resource that can be easily adapted to any discipline.[1] The *ALSM* lessons can be introduced in any sequence and may be used in a variety of ways: as an active introduction or dynamic closure to a unit of study; as a motivational, guided inquiry that supplements the core curriculum via application; or as an open-ended and independent investigatory project. Choose *ALSM* lessons that reflect and extend your required curriculum, or try one that looks appealing or taps into a particular student interest. Expand or modify the activities to meet your individual class needs and as time permits. Be mindful of opportunities that allow you to draw connections with past or future areas of study.

When implementing the lesson ideas, plan thoroughly but remain open to emergent and spontaneous learning opportunities, paying particular attention to student questions, impressions, and proposals. Student ideas are often the keys to establishing meaningful understanding and lasting motivation. Listen carefully to students as they investigate, think, and grow in confidence and knowledge. Take your cues from them as you brainstorm how to improve your instruction and seek ways to extend lessons into new areas of learning. Remember, successful teachers prepare thoroughly, enjoy the experience, and share their joy of learning with students.

This book is organized according to scientific discipline, as seen in the Table of Contents, to expedite the location of appropriate lesson ideas

---

1. Francis and Underhill (1996) provide another practical approach for developing interdisciplinary lessons, one that may be applied effectively in most classrooms. Their model relies on collaboration between two teachers (one math, one science), determines the key components of each topic to be taught, and uses a matrix format to plan instructional connections between those key components.

INTRODUCTION

for your curriculum planning. In actuality, the various disciplines overlap substantially and many activities include aspects of several diverse science disciplines. For example, Activity 17: Examining Colors, Color Perception and Sight, which is listed as a life science project, also involves a significant amount of physics. Similarly, most activities have a great deal more math embedded in the procedure than can be conveniently outlined in each lesson's list of processes and skills.

Take advantage of the curricular ambiguity inherent in linking disciplines, as it provides for more malleable lessons. The amount of science, math, art, literature, and so on that you include in your lesson depends on your pedagogic style, curriculum needs, and comfort level with the material. Students' backgrounds, interests, and goals should also come into play. In short, the depth and breadth of interdisciplinary connections is entirely up to you and your class, thus allowing for a customization of experience and meaning.

The *ALSM* lesson structure essentially provides a framework for students to do much of their own exploring and discovering. Start by introducing an idea or concept via a question, demonstration, or simple activity. This technique both engages your class and allows you to check for background knowledge and interest in the topic. Then, together with your class, proceed through the lesson, step-by-step. Students, who are often broken into small cooperative groups, collect, analyze, and discuss data, then share their reactions and insights. You have no particular script to follow, but modeling inquiry and problem-solving strategies in your own approaches to the activities is highly encouraged. The step-by-step directions are specific enough for you to easily work through the activity, yet general enough to allow for adaptations as necessary.

Assessment

Standardized or traditional assessment methods are usually inappropriate for evaluating integrated, problem-based tasks such as those that appear in this book. More suitable means of assessment have therefore been included for each lesson. These methods may be termed *authentic assessment*, or methods of evaluation that are well matched to experiential tasks. These methods include the following:

1. *Embedded assessment.* This technique blends assessment and instruction into a seamless whole, rather than following the traditional teach-test-teach-test format. In embedded assessment, you observe students as they participate in activities, looking for mastery of desired skills, processes, and content understanding. This sort of observation is facilitated by asking students questions about their experiences as they participate, such as "What if …?" or "Explain how you know…."

2. *Performance tasks.* Students apply their knowledge as they solve concrete problems in a procedure separate from the instruction sequence. For example, in Activity 8, students conduct an experiment comparing the jumping abilities of small, medium, and large origami frogs. You may assess their understanding of that experimental procedure by evaluating their performance as they test and analyze the jumping ability of a fourth, different size, frog.

3. *Journal entries.* Journals are an effective means of integrating language arts into the study of science and math. In their journals, students can collect and analyze data, explain what they have learned, and reflect on their experiences. Entries could also include illustrations and sketches, enabling you to assess from a nonverbal angle.

Specific assessment suggestions, and associated evaluation rubrics, are provided at the end of each lesson. To gain a more complete perspective of student progress, use several means of assessment within a given lesson. Whatever means of evaluation you choose, however, the assessment must match the instructional task, meaning that as you evaluate students in these wide-ranging investigations, you should do more than simply assess vocabulary acquisition and concept memorization with conventional techniques.

Safety Issues

During the implementation of the *ALSM* lessons, safety issues are of utmost importance. Use appropriate laboratory procedures while undertaking the activities, not only for the students' immediate safety, but also for the development of their lifelong safety habits. Specific safety considerations have been included for each lesson, and *The NSTA Ready-Reference Guide to Safer Science* (Roy 2007) is an excellent resource for further reading. Essential safety recommendations include the following:

1. Keep the work area clean. Clean up all spills immediately. Clean and store equipment and materials after use.

2. Never taste unknown chemicals. Always sniff gases cautiously. Store materials appropriately and safely.

3. Wear protective eyewear when working with hazardous substances or in any hazardous situations.

4. Be especially careful with electricity.

5. Provide constant supervision during individual or group work.

6. Allow sufficient time to complete tasks without rushing.

7. Provide sufficient lighting and ventilation.

8. Keep safety in mind when undertaking any ALSM or other investigatory activities.

It is vital to remember that "the best piece of safety equipment in your classroom is you—the informed adult shaping and controlling the learning environment" (Roy 2007, p. xiii).

Breaking Down Each Activity

The *ALSM* activity format is broken into a number of sections, each providing important information at a glance. Before trying the activity in class, read the entire lesson to facilitate choices of questioning strategies, modifications, assessment, and overall implementation. Practicing the activity ahead of time also minimizes mistakes and confusion during the classroom presentation. What follows is an explanation of each section of the activity format, as well as suggestions for use.

- **Overview:** A concise description of the activity that helps you determine where it may fit into your curriculum.

- **Processes/Skills:** A list of the processes and skills that students can be expected to employ as they participate in the lesson.

- **Recommended For:** A recommended grade range is provided for each lesson, but the lessons can be easily adapted for either younger or older students. In general, for younger students, simplify the use of terminology, eliminate or adapt procedures requiring fine motor skills, break the duration of the inquiry into shorter segments, and be sure that the lesson proceeds in a clear, orderly, and sequential manner. For older students, expand on the terminology and concepts, provide deeper connections to other disciplines, and offer opportunities for individual exploration, perhaps extending to investigations that can be undertaken outside the classroom (e.g., home, neighborhood, museums). A recommendation for individual, small group, or whole class instruction is also given.

- **Time Required:** An approximate time range for completion of the lesson that will, of course, vary from class to class and that should be considered only a rough estimate. Longer activities, or portions of activities, can be carried out over several days rather than all in one session.

- **Materials Required for Main Activity:** A list of just what materials are needed for the Main Activity as well as for any follow-up activities. Gather and, when necessary, assemble all materials prior to teaching the lesson—nothing ruins a well-organized plan as quickly as a missing item.

- **Connecting to the Standards:** A list of the standards related to the activity. The standards are also noted in the margins of the Step-by-Step Procedures at their main points of use, though they may well apply in several locations within a given activity. Complete discussions of each standard can be found in *National Science Education Standards* (NRC 1996) and *Principles and Standards for School Mathematics* (NCTM 2000).

- **Safety Considerations:** A warning of potential safety issues associated with the lesson. Familiarize yourself with classroom safety procedures and policies.

- **Activity Objectives:** A statement of performance objectives that students can be expected to reach during the lesson.

- **Background Information:** Conceptual information and explanations of terminology, when needed. In some cases, background information is included within the Step-by-Step Procedures.

- **Main Activity, Step-by-Step Procedures:** Sequential and ready-to-implement steps, which are adaptable to fit the needs of each classroom.

- **Discussion Questions:** A crucial aspect of the *ALSM* lessons is attention to your questioning strategy. Thought-provoking discussion questions are provided within the procedure and in this separate section following the procedure to promote the development of higher-order thinking skills, synthesis of disciplinary interconnections, and a deeper overall understanding. You should also develop your own queries, using a range of open- and closed-ended questions to stimulate students' critical thinking. Be careful not to dwell too much on or give away "the right answers," however, because an essential aspect of these lessons is that students have a chance to participate in the process of inquiry.

- **Assessment:** Several specific means of evaluating student progress and, in parentheses, suggestions for using the general method(s) of evaluation. Rubrics are provided for each lesson. In informal assessments, also include aspects of the affective domain, such as whether students are having fun and acting interested.

- **Going Further:** For some lessons, a connecting activity to expand the basic lesson into another subject area, particularly the visual arts.

- **Other Options and Extensions:** Additional ideas for extending the basic lesson. These can be pursued with the class as time allows, or they can be made available to individual students as homework, independent investigation, or a foundation for further study.

- **Resources:** Citations for articles, books, and other supplementary resources.

Final Thoughts

It is, indeed, possible to maintain high academic standards while "loosening up" your curriculum to include the natural connections among disciplines. Interdisciplinary connections are not simply interesting side trips; rather, they represent the foundation for lifelong understanding, curiosity, and problem solving. Science and mathematics reinforce each other, each discipline drawing upon the techniques and tools of the other and offering students experiences and awareness that are greater than the sum of the parts. By linking science with math we enhance comprehension and appreciation of both. Help students appreciate science and mathematics not just as topics to be studied in school, but as vital, interrelated elements of their everyday lives.

References

American Association for the Advancement of Science (AAAS). 1989. *Science for all Americans.* New York: Oxford University Press.

American Association for the Advancement of Science (AAAS). 1993. *Benchmarks for science literacy.* New York: Oxford University Press.

Fosnot, C. T. 1996. Constructivism: A psychological theory of learning. In *Constructivism: Theory, perspectives, and practice,* ed. C. T. Fosnot, 8–33. New York: Teachers College Press.

Francis, R., and R. G. Underhill. 1996. A procedure for integrating math and science units. *School Science and Mathematics* 96 (3): 114–119.

Lederman, N. G., and M. L. Neiss. 1998. 5 apples + 4 oranges = ? *School Science and Mathematics* 98 (6): 281–284.

McComas, W. F, and H. A. Wang. 1998. Blended science: The rewards and challenges of integrating the science disciplines for instruction. *School Science and Mathematics* 98 (6): 340–348.

Meier, S. L., G. Cobbs, and M. Nicol. 1998. Potential benefits and barriers to integration. *School Science and Mathematics* 98 (8): 438–445.

Meier, S. L., R. L. Hovde, and R. L. Meier. 1996. Problem solving: Teachers' perceptions, content area models, and interdisciplinary connections. *School Science and Mathematics* 96 (5): 230–237.

National Council of Teachers of Mathematics (NCTM). 2000. *Principles and standards for school mathematics.* Reston, VA: NCTM.

National Council of Teachers of Mathematics (NCTM). 2006. *Curriculum focal points for prekindergarten through grade 8 mathematics.* Reston, VA: NCTM.

National Research Council (NRC). 1996. *National science education standards.* Washington, DC: National Academy Press.

Piaget, J. 1970. *Genetic epistemology.* New York: Columbia University Press.

Roy, K. R. 2007. *The NSTA ready-reference guide to safer science.* Arlington, VA: NSTA Press.

Tobin, K., ed. 1993. *The practice of constructivism in science education.* Washington, DC: AAAS Press.

von Glasersfeld, E. 1993. Questions and answers about radical constructivism. In *The practice of constructivism in science education,* ed. K. Tobin, 23–38. Washington, DC: AAAS Press.

Vygotsky, L. S. 1978. *Mind in society.* Cambridge, MA: Harvard University Press.

Whitehead, A. N. 1929. *The aims of education.* New York: Mentor.

KEY INSTRUCTIONAL STRATEGIES USED IN EACH ACTIVITY

Activity	Hands-On	Minds-On	Guided Discovery	Experiment	Learning Cycle	Open-Ended Challenge	Project	Metacognition (Reflective Thinking)
1 Textures	X		X					
2 Visual Observation	X		X					X
3 TV		X						X
4 Möbius Band	X		X					
5 Alphabet Taxonomy	X		X					
6 Museum	X						X	X
7 Art Projects	X						X	X
8 Force and Motion	X			X				
9 Boats	X			X				
10 Magnets	X			X	X			
11 Chromatography	X		X			X		
12 Surface Tension	X		X	X				
13 Acids and Bases	X		X					
14 Soil	X		X					
15 Rocks	X		X			X		
16 Evaporation	X		X	X				
17 Colors	X		X		X			
18 Fingerprints	X		X			X		
19 Vegetable Prints	X		X				X	
20 Apple	X		X				X	

NATIONAL SCIENCE TEACHERS ASSOCIATION

+General Science

Activity 1
Investigating Textures

Overview

This simple but engaging activity about texture is for students in grades K–4. Textures are all around us, and they are important to our everyday activities—consider a piece of sandpaper, a cheese grater, or the soles of your shoes. As students become aware of the details and properties of familiar surroundings, which they do in this activity with their texture rubbings, they learn to more closely observe the conditions around them. Students also have the opportunity to recognize patterns, including mathematical associations, in their world.

Processes/Skills

- Observing
- Comparing
- Describing
- Identifying patterns
- Collecting
- Asking insightful questions

Recommended For

Grades K–4: Individual, small group, or whole class instruction
For K–1 students, focus on the collecting, comparing, and pattern discussion aspects only. For older students, add more math and art connections with the Going Further options.

Time Required

1–2 hours

Materials Required for Main Activity

- Paper (lightweight paper is best for making clear rubbings)
- Pencils (soft lead)
- Other writing utensils (e.g., charcoal, markers, or colored pencils)
- A range of objects with varying surface textures (e.g., sandpaper, corduroy cloth, Bubble Wrap, wood, leaves, a flower pot, rocks, shells, a cast-iron frying pan)

Materials Required for Going Further

- All of the materials required for the Main Activity
- Glue, paste, or glue sticks
- Student scissors

Connecting to the Standards

NSES
Grades K–4 Content Standards:
Standard A: Science as Inquiry

- Abilities necessary to do scientific inquiry (especially making good observations and communicating their ideas)
- Understanding about scientific inquiry (especially developing explanations using good evidence)

Standard B: Physical Science

- Properties of objects and materials (especially noticing the observable properties, such as textures, of objects and materials)

NCTM
Standards for Grades PreK–2, 3–5:

- Numbers and Operations (especially using number words, adding and/or multiplying, and estimating)
- Algebra (especially recognizing and describing patterns)
- Geometry (especially identifying, naming, and/or comparing two-dimensional shapes)

- Communication (especially analyzing, organizing, and expressing their thinking clearly to peers and teachers)

Safety Considerations

Basic classroom safety practices apply.

Activity Objectives

In the following activity, students

- collect and observe texture rubbings from a variety of surfaces;

- describe specific aspects of their rubbings and identify differences and similarities between the various rubbings; and

- clarify some of the ways that textures are important.

Main Activity, Step-by-Step Procedures

1. Begin by asking the class, "Can you think of some ways that the surface of the floor and the surface of the chalkboard (or any two surfaces in the room) differ?" Allow for a variety of student answers. Explain that one way the surfaces differ is in their texture and that texture is one property, or characteristic, of objects that we encounter. Explain that students will collect and compare the impressions of several different surfaces.

2. Demonstrate the rubbing process by placing a piece of paper over a flat, textured surface and gently rubbing a pencil or other writing utensil back and forth over the paper. An impression of the surface texture will appear in the pencil marks (if not, you may not be using a soft enough pencil, or you may be rubbing too lightly or too heavily). Ask students to make their own rubbings and check to see that they have mastered the technique.

3. With adequate paper supplies and pencils, instruct students to collect at least 10 different rubbings from the objects you have provided and from surfaces in the classroom (e.g., the wall, bulletin board, corrugated board, speaker cover). Encourage students to investigate as many types of surfaces as possible. Ask students, "What sorts of surfaces make the most interesting rubbings?" You may want to allow students to collect rubbings outside the classroom, too, if this is safe and feasible. On some surfaces (such as pavement, where there is a lot of variation) students may want to collect two or more rubbings from different areas.

SCIENCE
Properties of objects and materials

SCIENCE
Abilities necessary to do scientific inquiry

SCIENCE
Understanding about scientific inquiry

INVESTIGATING TEXTURES

MATH
Algebra
Communication

4. After all collections are complete, reassemble students in small groups to discuss, compare, and analyze the textural collections. The ensuing classwide discussion can focus on student-generated questions and ideas or the Discussion Questions offered below. Pay particular attention to patterns within and between the textural specimens collected. Younger students can analyze their collections by first cutting out (i.e., separating) the various specimens and then working in small groups to sort the cutouts based on their properties, such as whether the textures are bumpy or smooth, have repeating shapes, can be counted, and so on.

Discussion Questions

Ask students the following:

1. In your own words, describe three rubbings in detail, paying particular attention to textural patterns.

2. Are any of the rubbings similar to each other? How are they similar?

3. Which rubbings are most different from one another? What makes them different?

RUBRIC 1.1
Sample rubric using these assessment options

	Achievement Level		
	Developing 1	**Proficient** 2	**Exemplary** 3
Were students able to collect and describe a variety of textural rubbings?	Collected some rubbings but unable to describe them well	Collected and described rubbings effectively	Collected a wide variety of rubbings and were able to describe them in detail
Were students able to notice and describe similarities and differences between various rubbings?	Attempted to notice and describe similarities and differences between rubbings but unable to do so to any significant extent	Noticed and described adequately at least one similarity or difference between rubbings	Noticed and described extensively at least one similarity and one difference between rubbings
Were students able to identify any patterns in surface texture and/ or use?	Attempted to identify patterns in texture specimens but unable to do so to any significant extent	Identified at least one pattern in texture specimens	Identified multiple patterns in texture specimens and explained their implications
Were students able to explain how varying textures may be useful for different purposes?	Attempted to explain uses of varying textures but unable to do so to any significant extent	Explained the use, purpose, and/or value of at least one texture specimen	Explained in depth the use, purpose, and/or value of more than one texture specimen

4. Are any of the surface textures made that way for a particular reason (such as for added friction or greater smoothness)? How do you know?

5. What are some ways that textures are important to us in our daily lives?

Assessment

Suggestions for specific ways to assess student understanding are provided in parentheses.

1. Were students able to collect and describe a variety of textural rubbings? (Use Procedures 3 and 4 as performance tasks.)

2. Were students able to notice and describe similarities and differences between various rubbings? (Use Discussion Questions 1–3 during Procedure 4 as embedded assessments.)

3. Were students able to identify any patterns in surface texture and use? (Use all Discussion Questions during Procedure 4 as embedded assessments or use the Discussion Questions as prompts for science journal entries.)

4. Were students able to explain how varying textures may be useful for different purposes? (Use Discussion Questions 3 and 4 during Procedure 4 as embedded assessments or use those Discussion Questions as prompts for science journal entries.)

Going Further

To connect this texture inquiry to the visual arts, especially for older students, ask students to make a collage or mosaic of various rubbings. Cut and paste, using bits and pieces of rubbings. Students can make the collage even more interesting by using a variety of writing implements to create the rubbings. Consider having students depict an object or scene, portray a relationship between the various textures (e.g., alternating rough/smooth pattern), or represent any mathematical theme (an algebraic relationship such as $4 \times 5 = 5 \times 4$, a geometric shape such as small and large triangles, or an arithmetic representation such as simple textured cutouts of the numerals 1–5).

Other Options and Extensions

1. Homework: Ask students to collect interesting rubbings at home and bring them to class for further comparison, analysis, and discussion.

2. Mystery rubbings: Have students challenge one another with "unknown" rubbings, allowing their classmates to guess the source of the mystery rubbings.

MATH
Numbers and operations
Algebra
Geometry
Communication

MATH
Numbers and operations

3. Ask students to quantify the analysis by counting or estimating the number of bumps per square inch on several rubbings, using, for example, rubbings taken from the soles of several students' clean shoes. Students can add, multiply, or estimate depending on their skill levels and the nature of the textures being considered. Then by using a chart or bar graph format, students can compare the "feel" of the rubbings with the number of bumps per square inch. Ask students, "Do rough surfaces have more bumps per square inch than smooth surfaces? What do the numbers tell us?"

Resources

Edwards, L., M. L. Nabors, N.A. Branscombe, and M. Jones 2005. Science and social science in a nutshell. *Science and Children* 42 (6): 26–29.

Elliott, P. C. 2005. Algebra in the pre-K–2 curriculum? *Teaching Children Mathematics* 12 (2): 100–104.

McIntyre, M. 1978. Art experiences: Opening the door to science. *Science and Children* 15 (7): 38–39.

Miller, L. 1972. Creative rubbings. *School Arts* 72 (4): 4–5.

Schisgall, J. 1976. Discovering textures with young children. *School Arts* 76 (3): 16–17.

Small, T. 2006. On observation. *Science and Children* 43 (4): 45–46.

Ziemba, E. J., and J. Hoffman. 2006. Sorting and patterning in kindergarten. *Teaching Children Mathematics* 12 (5): 236–241.

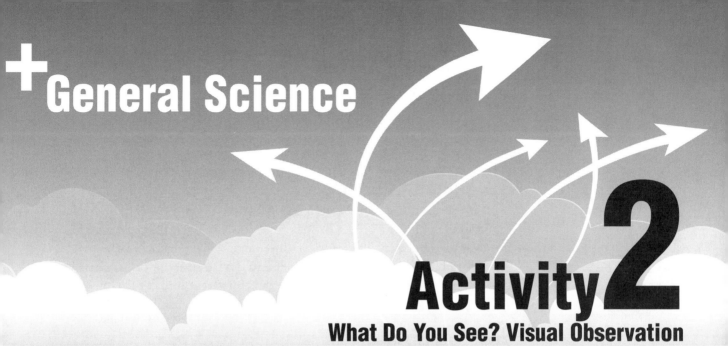

+General Science

Activity 2
What Do You See? Visual Observation

Overview

The famous New York Yankee catcher Yogi Berra once said, "You can observe a lot just by watching." This activity helps strengthen students' skills in a fundamental aspect of mathematics and science: visual observation. Students carefully examine and sketch a variety of objects, then analyze the sketches for shapes, patterns, and relationships. Students investigate the concept of "field of view" and learn how it can vary depending on distance from the object(s) being observed. As a Going Further activity, students incorporate careful observation, field of view, and shape/pattern recognition into a painting.

Processes/Skills

- Observing
- Measuring
- Collecting data
- Comparing
- Graphing
- Using a compass and ruler
- Using optical instruments
- Recognizing shapes and patterns
- Sketching
- Painting
- Cooperating
- Questioning

Recommended For

Grades K–4: Individual or small group instruction
For students in grades K–1, construct the viewfinders. Older students can take the measurements and conduct data analysis associated with Procedure 6, but you probably will need to demonstrate and explain the meaning of *field of view* for younger students without making the measurements in Activity Sheet 2.1 (p. 28).

Time Required

2–3 hours

Materials Required for Main Activity

- A variety of objects to observe (e.g., stapler, rocks, pinecones, seashells)
- Paper for drawing
- Pencils and/or other drawing tools
- Optical instruments (e.g., eyeglasses, hand lenses, binoculars, reversed binoculars, compound or dissecting microscopes)
- Drawing compass (for older students only)
- Student scissors
- Metric rulers
- Metersticks
- Large index cards
- Examples of paintings (student paintings or examples from art books or the internet) done at various distances (e.g., close-ups and landscapes)

Materials Required for Going Further

- Index viewfinder from Main Activity
- Paint (e.g., tempera, watercolors, fingerpaint)
- Paper for painting and drawing
- Other drawing materials as required (e.g., colored pencils, markers, crayons)

Connecting to the Standards

NSES
Grades K–4 Content Standards:
Standard A: Science as Inquiry

- Abilities necessary to do scientific inquiry (especially making good observations and communicating their ideas)

- Understanding about scientific inquiry (especially developing explanations using good evidence)

Standard B: Physical Science

- Properties of objects and materials (especially noticing the observable properties of objects and materials)

Standard E: Science and Technology

- Understanding about science and technology (especially how tools help with observations, and how different tools can be used to solve different problems)

NCTM
Standards for Grades PreK–2, 3–5:

- Algebra (especially recognizing and describing patterns)

- Geometry (especially identifying, naming, and/or comparing two-dimensional shapes)

- Measurement (especially understanding the attributes, techniques, and units of measuring)

- Problem Solving (especially applying strategies to solve a mathematical problem)

- Communication (especially analyzing, organizing, and expressing their thinking clearly to peers and teachers)

Safety Considerations
Basic classroom safety practices apply. Be particularly careful when using the drawing compass (as already noted, you will need to draw and cut the circles in Main Activity, Procedure 4, for younger students).

Activity Objectives

In the following activity, students

- observe and sketch a variety of familiar objects;

- observe and sketch using one or more optical instruments;

- define *observation* and *field of view* based on their own experiences in this lesson;

- measure field of view and recognize the relationship between field of view and viewing distance; and

- identify and describe patterns, colors, and geometric shapes in their observations, sketches, and paintings.

Main Activity, Step-by-Step Procedures

1. Begin by showing students an array of objects. This miscellaneous collection should include familiar objects (e.g., staplers, rocks, fast-food containers) as well as relatively or totally unfamiliar objects (e.g., pinecones, seashells, hand tools). Direct students to look at these objects for several minutes without speculation as to their use, origin, or impact. Tell students just to *look* at the objects, one at a time, and notice the details. Students should patiently concentrate on a few favorite objects, rather than rushing through the entire collection. Ask, "How do these objects differ? How are they similar? What visual characteristics can you observe? Which objects would you like to see more of? Why?" Encourage a discussion about observation: "Why do we see some things but not others? What does *observation* mean?"

2. Direct students to make detailed sketches of one or more of the objects using pencil, charcoal, crayon, or ink. You may want to suggest that students sketch other objects, indoor or outdoor views, and so forth in addition to the objects that you collected. Encourage attention to visual detail, shapes, patterns, and the "not so obvious," particularly with younger students. Ask students to try noticing something about the object that they have never noticed before. When each student has completed several sketches, ask them to identify patterns, colors, and geometric shapes in their work. Students may then share and discuss their sketches in groups.

3. Using the various optical instruments available, have students look at different objects and views to get the feel of the instruments.

SCIENCE
Abilities necessary to do scientific inquiry

SCIENCE
Properties of objects and materials

MATH
Algebra
Geometry
Communication

SCIENCE
Understanding about
  scientific inquiry
Understanding about
  science and technology

MATH
Measurement

Direct students to sketch one or more views, as seen through any particular instrument of choice. Ask, "Under what conditions might each of these instruments be useful? For instance, which might be good for close work? For distant viewing? How do you know?" Encourage a variety of responses.

4. Using a drawing compass and ruler, students can now make view-finders from index cards. To construct a viewfinder, students simply cut two separate holes, one 2 cm and the other 6 cm in diameter, in the index card (see Figure 2.1).

FIGURE 2.1. Viewfinder

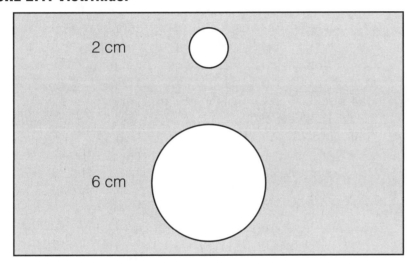

5. Working in pairs or small groups, with each student using her or his own viewfinder, students look through the large and small holes at near and distant objects (keeping the other eye closed). Students record rough sketches of what they see through the large hole, near and distant, and through the small hole, near and distant. Ask students, "How do the group members' large-hole sketches compare with one another? The small-hole sketches? How do the large-hole observations compare with observations made through the small holes?" These questions promote a variety of responses; encourage students to note that what they see through the viewfinder also depends on how far they hold it from their eye. Introduce the concept of *field of view* (that is, the entire area you can see at any given time and under any particular circumstances; the field of view can be relatively wide or narrow). Encourage students to define *field of view* for themselves.

SCIENCE
Understanding about
  scientific inquiry

MATH
Measurement
Problem solving
Communication

6. Next, working with partners, students measure and compare widths of fields of view. Ask, "How does the field of view change with distance from the object(s) being viewed?" In this case, the object is the chalkboard. Have one student from each pair stand 1 m from the chalkboard and hold their viewfinders 20 cm from their eyes (students should keep one eye closed). While remaining at that fixed distance, the students tell their partners where to make chalk marks on the blank chalkboard to indicate the width of the field of view as seen through the large hole, then through the small hole. They measure (in cm) and record the widths on Activity Sheet 2.1, page 28. Students then repeat the procedure at 2 m and 4 m away from the chalkboard. Have students consider what patterns they see in the data. (More advanced students may graph the distance versus width of field for each of the holes to clarify the relationship between these two variables.) Students should find that their field of view broadens as their distance from the chalkboard increases. Have students discuss their findings in groups. Engage the entire class in the discussion, using examples of paintings made at various distances to demonstrate the idea that field of view widens with distance.

Discussion Questions

Ask students the following:

1. What have you learned about your own ability to observe?

2. How can you become a better, more careful observer? How might observation skills affect your life?

3. Can you name some jobs that require careful observation skills?

4. How do the optical instruments change your field of view?

5. How did using the viewfinder affect your ability to observe?

Assessment

Suggestions for specific ways to assess student understanding are provided in parentheses.

1. Were students able to notice and sketch or describe details of the objects observed? (Use Procedures 1 and 2 as performance tasks and Discussion Questions 1 and 2 as an embedded assessment.)

2. Were students able to identify and describe patterns, colors, and geometric shapes in their paintings, sketches, and observations?

(Use Procedure 2 as a basis for embedded assessment observations, as a means of suggesting prompts for science journal entries, or as selected items in the student science portfolio.)

3. Were students able to observe and sketch using one or more optical instruments? (Use Procedure 3 as a performance task.)

4. Did students notice differences between unaided and aided observations, or between the various optical instruments? (Use Discussion Questions 3 and 4 as embedded assessments and/or as prompts for science journal entries.)

5. Could students generate working definitions of *observation* and *field of view?* (As an embedded assessment, ask for the definition of *observation* during Procedure 2 and the definition of *field of view* during Procedures 5 or 6. These definitions could also be requested in science journal entries after the activity ends.)

6. Were students able to measure field of view and recognize the relationship between field of view and viewing distance? (Observe students' implementation of Procedure 6, whether done via Activity Sheet 2.1 (p. 28) or by simple observation and analysis, as a means of embedded evaluation, or use Discussion Question 5 as a prompt for a science journal entry.)

RUBRIC 2.1
Sample rubric using these assessment options

	Achievement Level		
	Developing 1	Proficient 2	Exemplary 3
Were students able to notice and sketch or describe details of the objects observed?	Sketched but without great detail and could not discuss or describe details of sketches	Adequately noticed, sketched, and described details	Extensively noticed, sketched, and described details
Were students able to identify and describe patterns, colors, and geometric shapes in their paintings, sketches, and observations?	Attempted to identify patterns, colors, and geometric shapes, but unable to do so or to describe them to any significant extent	Identified and described at least one pattern thoroughly	Identified and described several patterns thoroughly
Could students generate working definitions of *observation* and *field of view?*	Used the two terms, but unable to offer specific definitions	Generated basic definitions of the two terms	Generated, used, and discussed definitions for the two terms

Going Further

To further connect this lesson to the visual arts, direct students to sketch several additional views in greater detail (and in color, if they choose), near or far, through small or large holes of the viewfinder. Remind students that for each sketch, they should record the approximate distance between viewfinder and eye and whether they used the large or small hole. If possible, allow students to leave the classroom to encourage a wider variety of observations. Students then choose one view and paint it. Consider using colors other than the "real" colors (tie this to a study of the Fauvist art movement by displaying copies of paintings by Matisse, Jawlensky, Derain, and Vlaminck). Also consider substituting shapes, patterns, and textures (e.g., triangle for circle, regular for irregular, rough for smooth). Display the student paintings. Discuss how students' paintings would have differed if they had incorporated a wider or narrower field of view.

Other Options and Extensions

1. Homework: Ask students to make sketches of objects or views at home (encourage parents to suggest objects). Share the sketches in class.

2. Consider Main Activity, Procedure 6: Challenge pairs or groups of students to use similar methods, or to devise new techniques, to investigate the relationship between width of field of view and the distance that the viewfinder is held from the eye. Ask, "How does the field of view change as you move the viewfinder closer to/ farther from your eye?" Encourage a variety of answers, and direct students to collect data to support or refute their explanations.

3. Create a writing assignment by asking students to describe their Going Further paintings in words (perhaps through a poem, story, newscast, or play).

4. Use a digital camera to take pictures with various fields of view. Show students the images and ask them to describe how the various photos differ in terms of information they convey.

Resources

Cook, H. M., D. P. Hildreth, and C. E. Matthews. 2004. "Hoeked" on science. *Science and Children* 41 (8): 42–47.

Gaylen, N. 1998. Encouraging curiosity at home. *Science and Children* 36 (4): 24–25.

Glatenfelter, P. 1997. Making observations from the ground up. *Science and Children* 34 (8): 28–30.

Glenn, D. 1984. Sight in stereo. *School Arts* 83 (9): 13–14.

Green, S., and J. Smith. 2005. Small things draw big interest. *Science and Children* 42 (4): 30–34.

Marsh, J., J. Loesing, and M. Soucie. 2004. Gee-whiz geometry. *Teaching Children Mathematics* 11 (4): 208–209.

Rommel-Esham, K. 2005. Do you see what I see? *Science and Children* 43 (1): 40–43.

Ziemba, E. J., and J. Hoffman. 2006. Sorting and patterning in kindergarten. *Teaching Children Mathematics* 12 (5): 236–241.

ACTIVITY SHEET 2.1
What Do You See? Visual Observation

Use this table to record the width of the field of view observed through the viewfinder (in cm), while holding the viewfinder 20 cm from your eye in each of the three cases. How does the field of view change with distance from the object(s) being viewed?

What do you predict?

Distance

	1 m	2 m	4 m
As viewed through large hole (6 cm)			
As viewed through small hole (2 cm)			

What conclusions can you reach about the effect of distance on your field of view?

+General Science

Activity 3
Science and Math on Television

Overview

Students certainly enjoy watching television, and they traditionally favor shows about science, mathematics, and technology. Consider the popularity of *MythBusters*, *Bill Nye the Science Guy*, *National Geographic Explorer*, and, of course, the old favorites *Watch Mr. Wizard* and *Mr. Wizard's World*. Why not combine schoolwork with that interest in watching television? In this activity students view a television show that they select themselves and not only examine its scientific, mathematical, and technological content but also reflect on their experience of viewing the show. The value of this straightforward activity lies in the development of media awareness and the cultivation of critical-thinking skills.

Processes/Skills

- Describing
- Analyzing
- Concluding
- Inferring
- Inquiring
- Communicating

Recommended For

Grades 2–4: Individual, small group, or whole class instruction
With grade 2 students, you can record a show yourself, watch it as a group, and expedite a discussion, with or without using Activity Sheet 3.1 (p. 34).

Time Required

1 hour

Materials Required for Main Activity

- Copies of Activity Sheet 3.1 for all class members

Connecting to the Standards

NSES
Grades K–4 Content Standards:
Standard A: Science as Inquiry

- Abilities necessary to do scientific inquiry (especially communicating and explaining their ideas)

Standard E: Science and Technology

- Understanding about science and technology (science is a way of explaining about the natural world)

Standard G: History and Nature of Science

- Science as a human endeavor (especially that science is undertaken by many different people who devote their lives to learning about phenomena in nature)

NCTM
Standards for Grades 3–5:

- Communication (especially analyzing, organizing, and expressing their thinking clearly to peers and teachers)

- Connections (especially noting the many interconnections between mathematics and science)

Safety Considerations
Basic classroom safety practices apply.

Activity Objectives
In the following activity, students

- choose, view, and reflect on an appropriate science-, math-, or technology-related television show;

- discuss the content and impact of the show; and

- explore how the show exemplifies science, technology, and/or mathematical investigation and understanding.

Main Activity, Step-by-Step Procedures

1. Ask students, "Who has seen a television show that has to do with science or math? Which show was it? Tell a partner what you liked about the show." You are bound to get a big response from students. Explain to students that they are to watch a television show of their choice and report back to the class on what they saw and what they thought about the show.

2. Instruct students to watch a television show based on science, math, technology, or a combination of the topics. They might also choose a mainstream show that uses science or mathematics in a significant way. For the sake of choice and variety, allow several days, even up to a week, for students to complete this assignment. During and after the show, students complete Activity Sheet 3.1 (p. 34) and prepare to discuss their observations and analysis in class. A brief note home to parents or guardians regarding the nature of the assignment is helpful. Another viable option is to record a show yourself, and then view, analyze, and discuss it as a group in class.

3. Students can initially share their findings in small, classroom discussion groups. Next, build on the individual analyses by examining the assignment with the entire class. Expand the discussion by posing a variety of open-ended questions: "What science was involved? What math was involved? Was technology involved, and if so, how? What would you change about the show? What did it make you wonder about? What did you learn by watching this show?" Help students see the various connections between science, technology, and mathematics, and clarify some of the ways that scientific investigations and careers are portrayed.

4. With older, media-savvy students you can explore reflective lines of questioning. Ask, "Did you agree with everything the show presented? If not, what did you disagree with and why? Who sponsored the show? Was the sponsor's product in any way related to the content of the show itself? Why do you suppose that particular sponsor decided to support this particular show (think of as many possible reasons as you can)?"

SCIENCE
Abilities necessary to do scientific inquiry

SCIENCE
Understanding about science and technology

MATH
Connections

SCIENCE
Understanding about science and technology
Science as a human endeavor

MATH
Connections

Discussion Questions

Ask students the following:

1. How were scientists and/or mathematicians portrayed on the show?

2. Did the show make math or science look like an attractive career possibility? Explain your answer.

3. Did you notice anything in the show that seemed wrong or inaccurate?

Assessment

Suggestions for specific ways to assess student understanding are provided in parentheses.

1. Did students choose, view, and reflect on an appropriate science-, math-, or technology-related television show? (Observe student responses during Procedure 3 or as you discuss the results of Activity Sheet 3.1 as an embedded assessment.)

2. Were students able to explain the content of the show, as well as discuss the show's impact on them? (Note the quality of student responses to the Discussion Questions as an embedded assessment.)

RUBRIC 3.1
Sample rubric using these assessment options

	Achievement Level		
	Developing 1	Proficient 2	Exemplary 3
Did students choose, view, and reflect on an appropriate science-, math-, or technology-related television show?	Chose and viewed a show, but little or no reflective analysis applied	Chose, viewed, and adequately reflected upon a show	Chose and viewed a show. Also reflected upon their own show, as well as the shows of others
Were students able to explain the content of the show, as well as discuss the show's impact on them?	Attempted to explain the content and impact but unable to do so to any significant extent	Effectively explained content and discussed impact of their show	Effectively explained content and discussed impact of their show and the shows of others

Other Options and Extensions

Record a television show or movie about science, math, or technology, and then undertake the following explorations with the class, using that recording:

Freeze Frame—Freeze the picture in random spots to observe in greater detail that particular "slice" of the show. Ask students, "What images are portrayed? What feelings are being encouraged in viewers? How does the frozen image promote the show's message?"

Get Up Close—Have students view the screen with a hand lens and describe the experience in words, or ask them to make a drawing, painting, or mosaic representation.

Get Far Back—Tell students to stand back at least 5 m from the screen and describe their impressions. Ask, "How does long-distance viewing change the experience of viewing?"

No Audio—Watch the video with the sound off for several minutes. Ask students to describe their impressions and explain how their impression of the show changes when it is only seen, not heard.

No Video—Cover the screen with a sheet of heavy paper and as a class listen to the show. Ask students to describe their impressions and how their impressions change when the show is only heard, not seen.

Resources

Cloke, G., N. Ewing, and D. Stevens. 2002. Light the math within. *Teaching Children Mathematics* 8 (5): 280–282.

Dubeck, L. W., S. E. Moshier, and J. E. Boss. 1988. *Science in cinema.* New York: Teachers College Press.

McLaren, P. 1995. *Critical pedagogy and predatory culture.* New York: Routledge.

SCIENCE AND MATH ON TELEVISION

ACTIVITY SHEET 3.1
Science and Math on Television

Choose a television show that is based on some aspect of science, math, technology, or some combination of those subjects. Watch the show and complete the analysis below.

1. Name of show:

Date and time of broadcast:

Channel:

Sponsors/Products:

2. Describe the show in three to five sentences. List any new words that you didn't understand.

_____

_____

_____

_____

3. Why did you choose this particular show?

_____

4. What science and/or math did you learn?

_____

_____

5. What did you like about the show? What would you want more of?

_____

_____

6. What didn't you like about the show? What would you change?

_____

_____

7. Rate the show on a scale of 1 to 10 (1 being the lowest). Would you recommend the show to a friend? Why or why not?

_____

_____

_____

_____

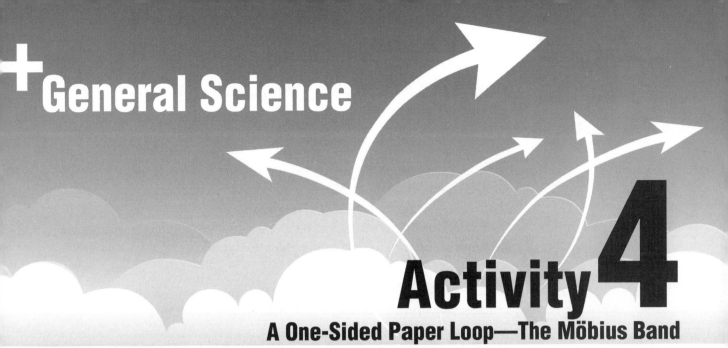

General Science

Activity 4

A One-Sided Paper Loop—The Möbius Band

Overview

What can you make from a sheet of paper that has only one side, where inside equals outside? The answer is a Möbius band, of course, the one-sided paper loop. In this activity, students in grades 3 and 4 explore a mathematical conundrum: How do we determine the number of sides an object has, and how can it be that this object has only one side? Through guided discovery, students find their own answers, making this a great lesson for developing their inquiry skills.

Processes/Skills

- Observing
- Comparing
- Describing
- Predicting
- Sketching
- Communicating
- Constructing
- Recognizing shapes
- Analyzing
- Developing spatial reasoning
- Inquiring
- Creating
- Cooperating

Recommended For

Grades 2–4: Small group or whole class instruction
For grade 2 students, you can make the Möbius bands ahead of time and offer more guidance as students explore the bands.

Time Required

1–2 hours

Materials Required for Main Activity

- Strips of newspaper (about 5 cm wide, prepared ahead of time)
- Glue sticks
- Student scissors
- Marking pens

Materials Required for Going Further

- Butcher paper
- Art supplies (for painting and drawing)
- Marking pens

Connecting to the Standards

NSES
Grades K–4 Content Standards:
Standard A: Science as Inquiry

- Abilities necessary to do scientific inquiry (especially making good observations, conducting a simple investigation, and communicating their ideas)
- Understanding about scientific inquiry (especially developing explanations using good evidence)

NCTM
Standards for Grades PreK–2, 3–5:

- Geometry (especially identifying, naming, and/or comparing two-dimensional shapes)

- Problem Solving (especially constructing new math knowledge through problem solving)

- Reasoning and Proof (especially developing, selecting, and evaluating arguments and proofs)

- Communication (especially analyzing, organizing, and expressing their thinking clearly to peers and teachers)

Safety Considerations

Basic classroom safety practices apply.

Activity Objectives

In the following activity, students

- decide how to determine whether a paper loop has one or two sides; and

- make a Möbius band and explore its properties.

Background Information

The Möbius band, named after its inventor, German mathematician August Ferdinand Möbius, has only one side and only one edge, and is known as a "nonorientable surface" in mathematical terminology. That is, it cannot be rotated to look like its own mirror image.

BFGoodrich patented conveyor belts in the shape of Möbius bands long ago because the belts use their inner and outer surfaces equally and therefore last twice as long as simple, looped belts. In fact, such belts are still commonly used in many industries, such as mining and manufacturing.

The Möbius band has also served as a model for high-performance, nonreactive electronic resistors; the shape allows the components to resist the flow of electricity without causing magnetic interference.

Interestingly, the chemical compound tetrahydroxymethylethylene, discovered in 1983, naturally takes the shape of a Möbius band making it a likely precursor to the development of other important biochemical compounds. For example, a cyclic protein called kalata B1, found in the African perennial plant *Oldenlandia affinis*, takes the Möbius shape, which makes the protein particularly stable, especially at high temperatures.

FIGURE 4.1.
Möbius band

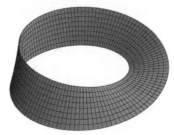

Main Activity, Step-by-Step Procedures

1. Show students a typical sheet of newspaper. Ask, "How many sides does this piece of paper have?" The expected answer is, of course, two. Next, cut a strip (about 5 cm wide) from the sheet of newspaper. Ask again, "How many sides does this piece of paper have?" The answer, again, is two. Cut another strip and glue the ends together, making a simple loop. Ask, "How many sides does the loop have?" Then ask, "*How do you know* how many sides the loop has?" Give each student group a loop to observe and handle, and allow them time to discuss and respond. Record student responses. Ask, "If a paper has two sides, and I want to make a continuous line with my marker on both, what do I have to do with the marker?" Help students see that you must *pick up the marker* at some point to make a continuous line. Have them try this in their groups, first with a flat sheet of paper and then with the loop. Do students agree that the "pick up the marker" test works to determine two sides?

2. Next, in front of the students, cut another strip from the newspaper and make a loop, but turn one end of the strip so that the top faces down before gluing. That is, put a twist into the loop. Ask once again, "How many sides does the loop have?" Students are likely to respond, "two." Ask, "How can we test for number of sides? Let's try the pick-up-the-marker test. What do you think will happen?" Record their responses. Now demonstrate the pick-up-the-marker test (an extra pair of hands will be helpful here). Students will be surprised when you never have to lift the marker to make a continuous line on what appears to be two sides of the loop. Ask students for their reactions to this demonstration. Explain that this special loop is called a Möbius band, after its inventor, August Möbius, a 19th-century German astronomer and mathematician. Keep the marked band to use in Procedure 4.

3. Let each student group make several Möbius bands of their own. The activity proceeds more smoothly if you provide precut strips of newspaper or butcher paper. For younger students, make the Möbius bands ahead of time, or at least assist students in making the bands. Encourage students to "explore" the band and to try the pick-up-the-marker (or pencil) test themselves. Ask students, "Is this what you would have expected? How do you explain this phenomenon?"

STANDARDS

SCIENCE
Abilities necessary to do
  scientific inquiry
Understanding about
  scientific inquiry

MATH
Problem solving

4. Return to your original Möbius band with the continuous line down the middle, used in Procedure 2. Ask, "What do you think will happen if I take my scissors and cut along the line that I drew on this band?" Record student responses and then try it out. The result will be a loop with a double twist in it. Ask students, "How many sides does this loop have? How can we find out?" Hopefully, students will suggest the pick-up-the-marker test, which you can try. Students will see that the loop has two sides. Let students try this, too, with their own Möbius bands.

5. Referring to your double-twist loop constructed in Procedure 4, ask students about the possible outcomes, facilitating a range of options: "What will happen if I cut along the line I drew on this loop? What are some possibilities? One simple loop? A simple loop with a double twist? With a triple twist? A Möbius band? Two Möbius bands? A double loop? Any other possibilities that you can think of?" Record student responses and then cut along the line. The result will be interlocking, twisted loops. Ask students, "Is either of these loops a Möbius band? Yes? No? *How do you know?*"

Discussion Questions

Ask students the following:

1. How can you explain the fact that the Möbius band has only one side? Can you think of any other objects or shapes that have only one side?

2. How might a belt shaped like a Möbius band be more practical than a simple loop in a belt-driven machine? (Both sides wear out evenly, as opposed to one side only, thus lengthening the life of the belt and saving money.)

3. How is a cycle (such as the yearly seasons, the water cycle, or a plant's life cycle) similar to a Möbius band? How is it different?

Assessment

Suggestions for specific ways to assess student understanding are provided in parentheses.

1. Could students determine that while a simple loop has two sides, the Möbius band has only one? (Observe students during Procedures 3–5 as performance assessment, and at the same time, listen to their responses to Discussion Question 1 as embedded evidence.)

2. Were students able to test and explore their own Möbius bands?

(Observe students during Procedures 3–5 as a performance assessment.)

3. Did students enjoy the activity? (As a form of embedded assessment, observe student reactions as the activity progresses. Are students enthusiastic? Are they exploring on their own? What sorts of comments and questions are students coming up with in their groups?)

RUBRIC 4.1
Sample rubric using these assessment options

	Achievement Level		
	Developing 1	Proficient 2	Exemplary 3
Could students determine that while a simple loop has two sides, the Möbius band has only one?	Attempted to explain but unable to do so	Explained and used the concept in Procedure 4 but unable to apply it in Procedure 5	Explained and used the concept effectively in Procedures 4 and 5
Were students able to test and explore their own Möbius bands?	Explored but did little or no testing	Explored and tested their bands	Explored, tested, explained, and discussed their bands effectively
Did students enjoy the activity?	Enthusiastic but not particularly well engaged in the activity	Enthusiastic and engaged in the activity	Enthusiastic, thoroughly engaged, and anxious to apply and discuss the activity

Going Further

For an art and science connection, students can make larger Möbius bands using strips of white butcher paper, approximately 25 cm wide and 1.5 m long. This activity can be undertaken by students working in groups, in pairs, or individually. Ask students to name some things that occur in time "loops," such as the seasons, the water cycle, the carbon cycle, or a plant or animal's life cycle. Ask students to choose one such cycle and illustrate it with a series of drawings or paintings on their large Möbius bands. Students will have to consider the number and width of their illustrations in order to have a good fit on the continuous loops. This project can be done in pastels, watercolor, or any other available, colorful materials. The completed cycle illustrations can be displayed by hanging them from the ceiling or by attaching them to a bulletin board.

Other Options and Extensions

1. Ask students to go home and demonstrate the amazing properties of the Möbius band to their families. Then ask students to

brainstorm, again with family members, some more practical applications of the band. Students may want to interview other adults to come up with ideas. Have students share their ideas in class and determine which are most useful, practical, innovative, and artistic. Which applications have the most to do with math? With science? With art? With some combination of math, science, and art?

2. Encourage students to research the life and work of August Möbius. What sort of man was he? How did he feel about his discovery?

Resources

Curran-Everett, D. 1997. The Möbius band: An unusual vehicle for science exploration. *Science and Children* 34 (4): 22–25.

Fleron, J. 1999. The Möbius metaphor. *Humanistic Mathematics Network Journal* 19 (9): 38.

Richardson, L. I. 1976. The Möbius strip: An elementary exercise providing hypotheses formation and perceptual proof. *The Arithmetic Teacher* 23 (2): 127–129.

Toll, D., and S. Stump. 2007. Characteristics of shapes. *Teaching Children Mathematics* 13 (9): 472–473.

General Science

Activity 5
Alphabet Taxonomy

Overview

Students constantly notice the world around them, and to help make sense of it all, they attempt to group and categorize objects and experiences they encounter. In science, the study of classification is referred to as *taxonomy*. To make this subject accessible and engaging for young learners, approach it from an interactive and relevant angle by allowing students to classify objects familiar to them. At the same time, students are encouraged to use many of the actual processes involved in scientific investigation and mathematical problem solving, including observing, measuring, describing, questioning, and communicating.

Processes/Skills

- Observing
- Classifying
- Creating
- Describing
- Analyzing
- Communicating
- Reasoning
- Recognizing shapes and patterns
- Cooperating

Recommended For

Grades K–4: Individual, small group, or whole class instruction

For students in grades K–1, you almost certainly will need to make up the alphabet and number cards yourself ahead of time and store them in envelopes.

Time Required

1 hour

Materials Required for Main Activity

- Assorted hardware (e.g., nails, screws, nuts, bolts, hinges)
- 8.5 in. × 11 in. photocopy paper
- Pens or pencils
- Student scissors

Connecting to the Standards

NSES
Grades K–4 Content Standards:
Standard A: Science as Inquiry

- Abilities necessary to do scientific inquiry (especially making good observations, using data to construct a good explanation, and communicating their ideas)

Standard B: Physical Science

- Properties of objects and materials (especially noticing the observable properties of objects and materials)

NCTM
Standards for Grades PreK–2:

- Algebra (especially recognizing and describing patterns)
- Problem Solving (especially constructing new math knowledge through problem solving)
- Reasoning and Proof (especially developing, selecting, and evaluating arguments and proofs)

Safety Considerations

Basic classroom safety practices apply.

Activity Objectives

In the following activity, students

- group letters and numbers into categories based on their shapes and explain their rationale for doing so; and

- define *taxonomy* in their own words and discuss the importance of classification to scientists and mathematicians.

Background Information

By comparing observable characteristics (known as *properties*) of a set of objects, scientists notice patterns, identify relationships, and differentiate among groups and individuals. In this way, meaning, context, and a sense of organization are constructed. Taxonomic principles are most often applied in science to the identification of plants and animals, but they are also widely used in other areas, including the categorization of chemical substances, microorganisms, rocks, and various physical phenomena. Mathematicians, too, must use classification schemes to identify prime numbers, negative integers, acute triangles, and so on.

Taxonomy is a subject worthy of consideration at the elementary school level. Taxonomic methods, activities, and concepts can be used in the classroom to promote logical, rigorous, and orderly thinking; to enhance the recognition of patterns and relationships; and to give students opportunities to effectively make more sense of the objects and experiences in their own lives. Although many types of objects can be successfully grouped by young children, you can begin by using the alphabet as your population of objects to be classified. Students already have experience with letters and their shapes, thus minimizing any anxiety or distraction due to the introduction of novel stimuli. Perhaps more important, by focusing on familiar objects in this introductory activity, the emphasis is placed on the process of taxonomy, rather than on the objects themselves. The observation and classification of the alphabetic shapes in this exercise can also encourage further literary and scientific proficiency.

Main Activity, Step-by-Step Procedures

1. Develop a context for the activity by clarifying and discussing with students the need for identification and classification. Begin by showing students an assortment of hardware pieces and asking them how they manage to tell the difference between these objects. Ask students, "Who might use these objects? Why would those people need to differentiate between them?" When holding up two different nails, for instance, ask, "What is similar about these

objects? What is different?" Explain that their various responses (e.g., longer, shorter, thicker, darker) are called *characteristics* of the nails (to simplify, you might substitute *things we notice* for *characteristics*; and for more advanced students, substitute *properties*).

Continue by asking students, "In what other situations do people need to tell the difference between one thing and another? What kinds of jobs involve this need? When do you yourself need to tell the difference between similar objects and how do you do so?" Tell students to consider the perspectives of different people, such as an author, doctor, recycler, carpenter, pilot, parent, and so on. Here is a great opportunity to weave in a book or story, such as *I Spy Funhouse* by Walter Wick and Jean Marzollo (1993), which reinforces observational skills, or *Uno's Garden* by Graeme Base (2006), a whimsical blend of observation, mathematics, and environmentalism.

2. Explain that scientists and mathematicians need to identify and classify things sometimes, just like everyone else, and that they use characteristics (or things they notice, or properties) of the objects to do so. Ask students, "What kinds of things might scientists need to classify or identify? Clouds? Rocks? Stars? Animals? What kinds of things might mathematicians need to classify or identify? Even and odd numbers? Ones, tens, hundreds? Shapes?"

   Write the word *taxonomy* on the chalkboard. Ask if anyone can define it in their own words, and explain that the activity students are about to do will help them understand better what the term means. Students will hopefully offer definitions such as "sorting," "classifying," or even "categorizing based on properties we observed." Of course, your emphasis on the actual terminology (e.g., *taxonomy*, *classification*, *grouping*, *characteristics*, and *properties*) will depend on the verbal backgrounds and readiness of your particular students. This activity is designed to strengthen process skills and therefore is not dependent on vocabulary background. That is, focus on the taxonomic process rather than just on vocabulary acquisition.

3. Working individually or in small groups, students first prepare their materials by folding a standard piece of 8.5 in. × 11 in. paper into a 6 in. × 6 in. box grid, that is, into 36 equal-size boxes. To fold the paper, students begin by folding it horizontally into thirds, like a letter, then fold that in half, still along the horizontal axis, making six columns. Then students open the paper and fold it again in the same manner, but in the opposite direction—along the vertical axis of the paper. This should make six columns in each direction, or 36

STANDARDS

boxes. For younger students, you may want to pre-line the papers or even make the letter and number cards ahead of time.

Next, instruct students to write a single capital, block letter in each box, beginning with the letter *A* and continuing through *Z*. In each of the 10 remaining boxes, students should write each of the digits 0 through 9. Students cut out the boxes along the creases and make two stacks of boxes—letters and numbers.

4. Setting the number boxes aside, students begin working with the letters alone. Ask them to arrange the letters into two piles (they do not have to be equal-size piles) based on some characteristic (or property) that they notice about the shapes of the letters. Tell students, "Don't consider the sounds that the letters make—just pay attention to the shapes—and *be sure that you can explain why you placed the letters into each of the two piles.*" As students complete this task, circulate around the room, asking them why they placed the letters as they did. When all are finished, allow several volunteers to explain their classification schemes, enabling everyone to see that there are many plausible ways to separate the letters. Point out that their classification schemes (the ways that they sorted the letters into two separate piles) are based on patterns of similarities and differences.

5. Students should combine the letters again into a single pile. Instruct them to separate the letters into three stacks this time, based again on some observable characteristic. Proceed as you did in Procedure 4, but leave the letters sitting in the three arranged piles. When all are finished, allow several volunteers to explain their classification schemes, paying particular attention to their reasoning and description of patterns observed.

6. Next, each student or student group should retrieve the stack of numerical digits and place each square onto the appropriate stack of letters, using the same classification scheme they invented in Procedure 5. Because students are looking at shape alone, they should be able to classify each numeral based on its form alone, just as they did with the letters. The numbers act here as a set of unknowns that students must separate using a previously defined taxonomic scheme (a scheme that each student was allowed to create). When everyone is finished with this task, ask for volunteers to explain how their systems worked, again pointing out that though their individual taxonomic schemes may have been quite different, the various systems still worked. Explain that there are many ways to classify things; the system they chose depended on what

SCIENCE
Abilities necessary to do scientific inquiry
Properties of objects and materials

MATH
Algebra
Problem solving
Reasoning and proof

they observed and what they wanted to accomplish. Occasionally, however, a numeral won't fit easily into a particular scheme. If this occurs, explore with students the reason or reasons for its exclusion from the three letter stacks and discuss how the scheme might be modified to appropriately accommodate all of the digits. If modification is not feasible, students may need to add another stack, just as scientists have to do if they discover an entirely new species of animal or plant.

Now ask students to explain, either orally or by writing in their science journals, their understanding of the term *taxonomy* and why it might be a useful word.

Discussion Questions

Ask students the following:

1. Gold miners and geologists both must classify rocks, but because they have different needs and goals, they might use different taxonomic schemes. Consider their needs and goals, then describe rock classification schemes for each to use and explain how the two schemes differ.

2. When you added the numerals to the three stacks of letters, were there any difficulties? That is, did all the numbers fit into your taxonomic scheme? If not, which one(s) didn't fit and why not?

3. What sorts of things do you classify in your own life, and what properties do you use to classify them?

Assessment

Suggestions for specific ways to assess student understanding are provided in parentheses.

1. Were students successful at grouping letters into two and three categories based on observable shape-related properties? Were they also able to successfully add the numerals to the three-stack scheme? (Use Procedures 3 and 4 as performance assessments and students' verbal responses to Discussion Question 2 as an embedded assessment.)

2. Were students able to describe what is meant by the term *taxonomy*? (Listen to students' verbal responses to this question as part of Procedures 4 and 5 as an embedded evaluation, or use this question as a prompt for science journal entries.)

3. Did students recognize the importance of taxonomic classification

to scientists and mathematicians? (Use students' responses to Discussion Questions 1 and 3 as an embedded assessment or as prompts for science journal entries.)

RUBRIC 5.1
Sample rubric using these assessment options

	Achievement Level		
	Developing 1	Proficient 2	Exemplary 3
Were students successful at grouping letters into two and three categories based on observable shape-related properties?	Grouped the letters but could not clearly explain their reasoning for doing so	Grouped the letters and could explain and discuss their reasoning for doing so based on their understanding of the letters' properties	Grouped the letters, could explain their reasoning, and could compare their pattern to the patterns of other groups using other grouping schemes
Were students able to successfully add the numerals to the three-stack scheme?	Were engaged in the task but could not successfully add the numerals to the appropriate stacks	Successfully added the numerals to their own three-stack scheme	Successfully added the numerals to their own three-stack scheme and were able to do so using other groups' schemes as well
Were students able to describe what is meant by the term *taxonomy*?	Attempted to define *taxonomy* in their own words but were not accurate	Successfully defined *taxonomy* in their own words	Successfully defined *taxonomy* in their own words and were able to discuss associated patterns and their reasoning in this activity
Did students recognize the importance of taxonomic classification to scientists and mathematicians?	Attempted to discuss the implications of taxonomic classification but were unable to do so to any significant extent	Recognized the importance of taxonomic classification to scientists	Recognized the importance of taxonomic classification to scientists and mathematicians

Other Options and Extensions

1. Ask students to separate the letters based on the sounds that they make, which are observable, auditory properties.

2. Encourage students to extend the processes of taxonomy to piles of leaves from different trees or even from the same tree (discernible differences exist between leaves from the same tree), animal photos, shell collections, rock collections, books, foods, tools, miscellaneous household items, and so on. As students do this, have them explore the idea that some systems of categorization are more appropriate

and useful than others, depending on what one wishes to accomplish. For instance, a scientist studying volcanoes might want to arrange a rock collection into "volcanic" and "nonvolcanic" groups, whereas a miner might consider "rocks that contain ore" and "rocks that do not contain ore." The volcanologist's scheme is not necessarily appropriate and useful for the miner, and vice versa.

3. Promote the quantification of observable properties by introducing measuring instruments such as metric rulers, scales or balances, and thermometers into the taxonomic process.

4. Encourage students to look individually, with friends and family, for ways that they currently categorize items in their own lives. Help students discover new items and new, more effective means of classification.

References

Base, G. 2006. *Uno's garden.* New York: Abrams Books for Young Readers.

Wick, W., and J. Marzollo. 1993. *I spy funhouse.* New York: Cartwheel.

Resources

Crowther, D. T. 2003. Harry Potter and the dichotomous key. *Science and Children* 41 (2): 18–23.

Elliott, P. C. 2005. Algebra in the pre-K–2 curriculum? *Teaching Children Mathematics* 12 (2): 100–104.

Gaylen, N. 1998. Encouraging curiosity at home. *Science and Children* 35 (4): 24–25.

Gotsch, H., and S. Harris. 1990. Backyard taxonomy. *Science and Children* 27 (4): 25–27.

Small, T. 2006. On observation. *Science and Children* 43 (4): 45–46.

Stemn, B. S., and J. E. Collins. 2001. Do numbers have shapes? *Teaching Children Mathematics* 7 (9): 542–547.

Whiten, D. J., and P. Whiten. 2003. Talk counts: Discussing graphs with young children. *Teaching Children Mathematics* 10 (3): 142–149.

+ General Science

Activity 6
Your Very Own Museum—Making Collections

Overview

Much more than childish pastimes, collections form the basis for museums of natural history, found object art projects, and personal hobbies. Furthermore, many notable scientists—Charles Darwin, for example—began their lifelong investigations with childhood collections. In this activity, students choose a category and collect specimens from the natural world, gathering as wide a range of those objects as possible. Students then analyze and compare the specimens within their personal collection. Also, each student contrasts the breadth, depth, and patterns of her or his collection with those of other students.

Processes/Skills

- Observing
- Describing
- Communicating
- Comparing
- Reflecting
- Recognizing shapes, patterns, and relationships
- Appreciating
- Creating
- Problem solving

Recommended For

Grades K–4: Individual, small group, or whole class instruction
This activity is easily adapted for learners in grades K–1 by assisting them as they consider areas of interest; keeping the vocabulary simple and concrete; offering assistance with the collecting, displaying, and presenting

process; allowing them to collect as a group; and encouraging family members to help children with the activity.

Time Required
Open-ended; will vary depending on the nature and extent of the collection

Materials Required for Main Activity
- Will vary greatly depending on the nature of the collection

Materials Required for Going Further
- General art supplies (These will vary with student and teacher interest but may include paper, paint, clay, scissors, and glue.)

Connecting to the Standards

NSES
Grades K–4 Content Standards:
Standard A: Science as Inquiry

- Abilities necessary to do scientific inquiry (especially making good observations and communicating their ideas)
- Understanding about scientific inquiry (especially that scientists use different sorts of investigations, including collections, to understand the world around them)

Standard B: Physical Science

- Properties of objects and materials (especially noticing the observable properties of objects and materials)

NCTM
Standards for Grades PreK–2, 3–5:

- Numbers and Operations (especially understanding and using numbers, operations, and estimation)
- Algebra (especially recognizing and describing patterns)

Safety Considerations

Basic classroom safety practices apply. Be particularly careful to avoid toxic vegetation, biting or stinging insects and spiders, and any other potentially hazardous collectibles.

Activity Objectives

In the following activity, students

- collect objects or materials from their chosen category from the natural world;

- make meaningful connections between their collections and math, science, and related careers; and

- identify and analyze patterns and relationships among their specimens, compare the collection's properties, and reflect on the collecting process.

Main Activity, Step-by-Step Procedures

1. The value of this relatively simple activity lies not only in the collecting but also in the wondering, discovering, and extending. Therefore, the crucial aspects of collecting are (a) making sure that all students have *selected a subject of interest to them,* and (b) following up on student collecting efforts with a variety of questions, inquiries, and projects that prompt them to reflect meaningfully on their collections. These collections can be short-term or ongoing throughout the school year. Several ideas are presented here, but teachers are encouraged to adapt to students' concerns and directions.

2. Begin the activity by asking students if they already collect things and, if so, what they collect. Responses are likely to be varied and enthusiastic. Next, have the class brainstorm objects from nature that can be collected. A class trip to a natural history museum will certainly raise interest and expand the range of student-generated possibilities. What sorts of objects or materials would they like to collect? How feasible are their ideas? (If the objects are not readily available, students are likely to grow frustrated and bored quickly.) The class may choose to all focus on a particular category of specimens, students may work together to form group collections, or individuals may gather objects on their own. Again, because of the simplicity of the activity, the possibilities are endless, and student choice is the key factor.

STANDARDS

SCIENCE
Abilities necessary to do
  scientific inquiry
Understanding about
  scientific inquiry
Properties of objects and
  materials

MATH
Numbers and operations
Algebra

3. Students may choose a particular type of object for any number of reasons: interest, past experience, beauty, or curiosity. There is no "wrong" rationale. Again, it is important that students find topics of personal interest to them. A variety of reference books and magazines may help reluctant students identify subjects of interest. Possible collections include ants in a jar (or an ant farm), photos or sketches of clouds, rocks, seashells, soil samples, water samples, algae, flying insects, flowers and vegetation (pressed or dried), recordings of environmental sounds, casts of animal tracks, recordings of bird songs, spiders, spider webs, fossils, fungi, insects found around the home, pinecones, small pieces of tree bark, photos or sketches of geological formations, wood, eggs, or feathers. Having some of these, or other, options available in the classroom for student observation is likely to encourage interest, especially for younger students. As already stated, it is imperative that students avoid harmful collectibles.

4. Some collections may require special equipment (e.g., a butterfly net, which can be made easily and inexpensively at home); others may require extra internet or library research. This is an excellent opportunity for students to find out more about their topics, implement trial-and-error analysis, and begin to discover what it means to do scientific fieldwork. Special techniques will emerge from research and practice. For instance, spider webs can be collected on black paper by first spraying the web lightly with spray starch.

    Organization and display will vary depending on student age, ability, and the nature of each collection. Collections may, for instance, be presented in small boxes, glued to tagboard, or arranged as hanging mobiles. Encourage creativity, but be sure that the displays promote thoughtful consideration and organization of the collections.

5. Some collections (e.g., bird eggs or pinned insects) may raise issues of ethical treatment of the living environment. Some students may oppose such invasive collections on moral grounds. Student perspectives should be respected, encouraged, and developed in individual writing assignments, small-group discussions, and classwide, nonjudgmental dialogue. If any collections involve living specimens (whether plant or animal), you must be certain that the organisms are treated kindly and are cared for properly in terms of their unique needs, before returning them unharmed to their natural homes. Tell students not to take items such as webs, eggs, and nests that are still viable and in use (students must check with an adult beforehand if there is any question). Challenge students to make as

little environmental impact as possible. This is an excellent opportunity for students to gain firsthand experience as to what *environmental impact* means.

6. After students complete their collections, have them present, display, and discuss their collections with classmates. Focus discussions on the identification of mathematical patterns and relationships within and between collected specimens. Ask students, "How do various specimen measurements compare? What color patterns can you identify? How do the shapes compare? Count and compare the number of parts (e.g., the number of pistils in collected flowers). What percentage or fraction of the collection displays a certain property (e.g., what percentage of the seashells were spiral shaped)?" You may designate a special table or area in which collection samples may be displayed. Such a table makes a wonderful learning center for individual or group work. Help students determine what types of scientists collect specimens and exactly what they collect. Examples include scientists who study plants, animals, weather, and stars. Ask students, "Can collections contain photos, drawings, recordings, and casts, or must they only contain actual objects? How might collections be helpful to scientists in their studies?"

Discussion Questions

Ask students the following:

1. Why did you choose to make this particular collection? What about it appealed to you?

2. What mathematical ideas do you see represented in your collection or the collections of other students? Consider number, shape, and pattern.

3. How does your collection compare with the collections of other students? Consider number of specimens, variety of specimens represented, difficulty of collecting these particular specimens, how they are presented, and so on.

4. What did you know about your specimens before you started the collection? What have you learned about your specimens and about collecting in general?

5. What jobs, careers, or professions might be associated with the specimens that you collected? Have you considered pursuing those careers? Explain.

Assessment

Suggestions for specific ways to assess student understanding are provided in parentheses.

1. Were students able to successfully collect items? Were the collections wide-ranging and innovative? (Notice the extent of students' collections as they are accumulated as performance assessment.)

2. Were students able to make meaningful connections between their collections and mathematics or science investigations and related careers? (Listen to their responses to Discussion Questions 1, 3, 4, and 5 and use these as embedded assessments or as prompts for science journal entries.)

3. Did students identify, compare, and analyze patterns and relationships within and between collections, including a comparison of the collection's properties, and discuss the collecting process? (Listen to their responses to Discussion Question 2 as an embedded assessment or as a prompt for science journal entries.)

RUBRIC 6.1
Sample rubric using these assessment options

	Achievement Level		
	Developing 1	Proficient 2	Exemplary 3
Were students able to successfully collect items?	Collected a few items but either not extensively or with no particular focus	Collected a reasonable number of items within a particular topic focus	Collection was extensive, focused, and clearly displayed
Were students able to make meaningful connections between their collections and mathematics or science investigations and related careers?	Attempted to make connections but unable to do so to any significant extent	Could explain the value of collections for science and math investigators	Could explain the value of collections for science and math investigators, and could discuss the value of collections to specific science and math careers
Did students identify, compare, and analyze patterns and relationships within and between collections, including a comparison of the collection's properties, and discuss the collecting process?	Attempted to determine patterns and relationships within their collection but unable to do so to any significant extent	Able to identify, compare, and analyze patterns and relationships within their collections	Able to identify, compare, and analyze patterns and relationships within their collections, and also between various collections

Going Further

Allow students to create a sketch, drawing, painting, ceramic, collage, sculpture, mobile, or other art project based on some aspect or aspects of their specimens. Promote innovation and divergent thinking. Ask students to explain their project in a written journal entry. Display the projects gallery style when completed. Invite parents, administrators, other teachers, and students to visit the gallery. Collect visitor responses in writing (make pencils and paper available to all visitors) and post the comments on a bulletin board. Invite your students to consider the "public" reaction to their work.

Other Options and Extensions

1. Students can conduct a mathematics-related investigation or project (individually, in small groups, or as a class) relating to their collections. Counting, averaging, identifying patterns and relationships, weighing and measuring, identifying geometric shapes, problem solving, and constructing tables or graphs are all possible directions. Projects should include conclusive interpretations of any mathematical results (data) obtained. Then students can apply their results and conclusions to other situations, collections, and experiences. For example, if students collect a number of dried flowers, they might count the petals on each and find the average number of petals within their collections. Students might also make a bar graph of the petal counts (e.g., two flowers had five petals, three had six, and so on). Then they could use their results to predict how many petals were on the flowers in another student's flower collection.

2. Students can write poems, which can include haiku and limericks, about collections or particular specimens.

Resources

Ashbrook, P. 2006. Communicating about collections. *Science and Children* 44 (3): 18–19.

Gaylen, N. 1998. Encouraging curiosity at home. *Science and Children* 36 (4): 24–25.

McIntyre, M. 1977. Collections. *Science and Children* 15 (1): 38–39.

Schwerdtfeger, J. K., and A. Chan. 2007. Counting collections. *Teaching Children Mathematics* 13 (7): 356–361.

Van Deman, B. A. 1984. The fall collection. *Science and Children* 22 (1): 20–21.

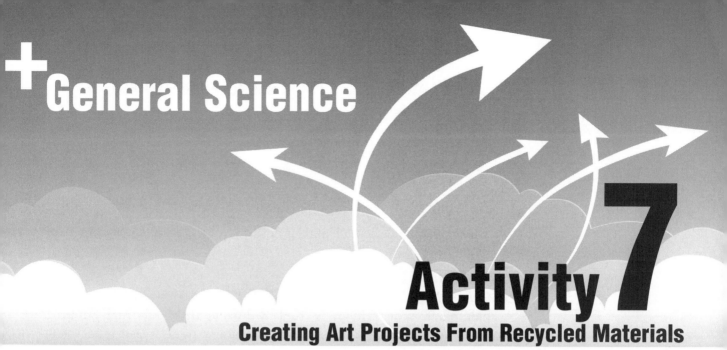

General Science

Activity 7
Creating Art Projects From Recycled Materials

Overview

So you have gotten your students to recycle paper, aluminum, and plastic, but you want to take it one step further. Why not challenge students to design a collage, mosaic, or shadowbox entirely from "found objects"— recycled, natural, and discarded materials? Found object art has a history dating back to prehistoric times. The aesthetic nature of the art of salvage connects students not only to ancient, creative roots, but also to a future in which we must learn to reduce, reuse, and recycle. According to Stribling, "The Found Artist occupies a unique spot in the world of art for he [or she] is both a *collector* of things and a *creator* of things" (1970, p. x). Stribling also noted that the collector/creator's "delight in finding treasures in unexpected places is compounded by the satisfaction of 'refinding' them in his [or her] mind and imagination" (1970, p. x). As "refinders" of often overlooked materials, students develop a deeper and very practical understanding of conservation and environmentalism. When we compound that experience by adding a mathematical theme to the art projects, we have a truly interdisciplinary lesson.

Processes/Skills

- Observing
- Comparing
- Describing
- Identifying shapes and patterns
- Collecting
- Enjoying
- Communicating
- Problem solving

- Reflecting
- Creating
- Recognizing mathematical relationships

Recommended For

Grades K–4: Individual, small group, or whole class instruction
Accommodate students in grades K–1 by dividing them into small groups, providing additional assistance, and encouraging parents to assist their children with this activity.

Time Required

2–3 hours

Materials Required for Main Activity

- A wide variety of discarded and recycled objects and materials (e.g., empty egg cartons, empty milk cartons, magazines, newspapers, cloth, twine, aluminum, foil, plastic containers)
- A wide variety of natural objects and materials (e.g., vacated birds' nests, colored pebbles, sand, feathers, shells, rocks, seed pods, leaves, bark)
- Student scissors
- Construction paper
- Glue, paste, or glue sticks
- Paints, clay, and other basic art supplies as needed

Connecting to the Standards

NSES
Grades K–4 Content Standards:
Standard B: Physical Science

- Properties of objects and materials (especially noticing the observable properties of objects and materials)

Standard C: Life Science

- Organisms and environments (especially the concept that all organisms, including humans, cause changes in their environments, and those changes can be harmful or helpful)

NCTM
Standards for Grades PreK–2, 3–5:

- Numbers and Operations (especially understanding and using numbers, operations, and estimation)

- Algebra (especially recognizing and describing patterns)

- Measurement (especially understanding units and processes of measurement and measurable aspects of objects)

- Communication (especially analyzing, organizing, and expressing their thinking clearly to peers and teachers)

- Representation (especially using representation to record and communicate mathematical ideas)

Safety Considerations
Basic classroom safety practices apply.

Activity Objectives
In the following activity, students

- select and collect a variety of usable "found" objects and materials and use those materials to create imaginative collages, mosaics, and shadowboxes;

- incorporate mathematical patterns (algebraic, geometric, and arithmetic) into their art projects; and

- expand their understanding of the value of discarded, recycled, and natural objects and materials.

Main Activity, Step-by-Step Procedures

1. Begin by showing the class a variety of discarded and/or recyclable materials. Ask students to think about what these objects and materials have in common and what the objects have been typically used for. Ask, "How do these objects and materials change our environment? Are they helpful or harmful?" (Encourage divergent and creative answers.)

2. Next, show students a variety of natural objects and materials. Ask them to think about what these objects and materials have in common. Ask students, "What were the objects and materials typically used for? What else could they possibly be used for?" (Again, encourage divergent and imaginative, even playful, answers.)

SCIENCE
Organisms and
environments

CREATING ART PROJECTS FROM RECYCLED MATERIALS

SCIENCE
Properties of objects and
  materials

MATH
Numbers and operations
Algebra
Measurement
Representation

MATH
Communication

3. If they don't suggest the idea themselves, explain to students that the discarded and natural materials could be used in art projects (materials and ideas might also be found in students' personal collections as explored in Activity 6, p. 51). The first step is to gather materials for use. Encourage students to bring in cleaned recyclable/reusable objects and natural materials from their neighborhoods or homes. They will use the materials they gather. Give them several days to amass an adequate collection. You may want to augment their collections with interesting materials that you find.

4. When sufficient materials have been collected, show students examples of collages, mosaics, and shadowboxes that you or past students have created. So that students don't just mimic your examples, be sure to have them generate specific ideas about what they could do differently to make their art projects unique and meaningful. Be sure to draw their attention to the mathematical patterns represented in each project example. Inform students that each of their projects—no matter its content, subject matter, or theme—*must* incorporate a mathematical pattern. Patterns can be geometric (e.g., spiral, square, circular), arithmetic (e.g., small to large, two-by-two, depictions of a particular number with different objects), or natural (e.g., bilateral symmetry of the colors in a butterfly's wings or the radial symmetry of a starfish). An interesting pattern possibility for an egg carton shadowbox is algebraic: Students can depict equivalencies for a particular number in each of the egg compartments (e.g., four: two plus two, or three plus one, or four plus zero) or for particular types or colors of seeds in shadowbox holes (e.g., two light and two dark in one hole, three light and three dark in another, four light and four dark in the next, and so on). Give students a few minutes in small work groups to note math patterns they might like to use and how they might want to implement them with the available materials. Provide time for the groups to share and exchange ideas.

5. Collages and mosaics can be built on construction paper, cardboard, or even pieces of plywood. They can include written words, other media (such as watercolors or clay), or a background of magazine photographs. Cooperative groups can build large mosaics or collages. Shadowboxes can be made easily from the bottom half of egg cartons. Students can cut off the carton's top (and recycle it or use it as material for this or another project), paint the bottom half of the carton, and fill in the 12 holes with a depiction of a mathematical pattern, using small objects such as pebbles,

seeds, buttons, magazine pictures, and so on. The sky is the limit with these projects. The only boundaries are time and materials. In addition to the mathematical pattern, the project could also include a science theme (such as cell division, evolution, plant growth and development, or environmentalism). As you circulate through the room, be sure that students can explain their mathematical patterns when asked; assist and check for engagement and comprehension.

6. When all projects are complete, hold a Found and Discarded Object Art Gallery showing in which students display and discuss their work, particularly the patterns within their projects, with one another. Invite other school community members—including parents, administrators, other teachers, and students—to your room to view and discuss the projects with the artists. Obtain student-artist consent before showing any of the work; this should be entirely voluntary and fun, not coerced.

Discussion Questions

Ask students the following:

1. What normally happens to discarded/recycled and natural "found" materials?

2. If you were to create another collage, mosaic, or shadowbox, what would you do differently? Why?

3. What other mathematical patterns could you portray, and how would you portray them?

4. Make a list of other objects or materials that you would like to use in such a project.

5. Why do you think that so many objects and materials are thrown away or overlooked when they can be put to good use?

Assessment

Suggestions for specific ways to assess student understanding are provided in parentheses.

1. Were students able to select and collect a variety of usable materials and objects, and did they use those materials to create imaginative collages, mosaics, or shadowboxes? (Use embedded observations during Procedures 3–6 as performance assessment evidence.)

2. Did students create mathematical patterns (algebraic, geometric,

and arithmetic) using the materials and objects collected, and could they explain their patterns? (Use embedded observations during Procedures 3 and 4 as performance assessment evidence and Discussion Question 3 as a prompt for a science journal entry.)

3. Did students expand their understanding of the value of discarded, recycled, and natural objects and materials? (Use student responses to Discussion Questions 1, 2, 4, and 5 as embedded evaluations and as prompts for science journal entries.)

RUBRIC 7.1
Sample rubric using these assessment options

	Achievement Level		
	Developing 1	Proficient 2	Exemplary 3
Were students able to select and collect a variety of usable materials and objects, and did they use those materials to create imaginative collages, mosaics, and/or shadowboxes?	Found a few materials but were not able to create an adequate art project	Found a reasonable number of materials and created a thoughtful art project	Found and used a substantial number and variety of materials with which to make a particularly creative art project
Did students create mathematical patterns (algebraic, geometric, and arithmetic) using the materials and objects collected, and could they explain their patterns?	Attempted but were unable to create math patterns within their found object art pieces	Created math patterns within their found object art pieces and explained those patterns	Created math patterns within their found object art pieces and explained those patterns, as well as compared their patterns to those of other students' projects
Did students expand their understanding of the value of discarded, recycled, and natural objects and materials?	Understanding improved little	Understanding improved considerably	Understanding improved substantially, and grew to include a strong interest in the topic

Other Options and Extensions

1. Students can tie this activity into an expanded exploration of recycling, reducing, and reusing.

2. Students can investigate the ancient, multicultural origins, and history of found object art. Encourage students to learn about the work of well-known found object and natural materials artists, such as Marcel Duchamp, Robert Rauschenberg, and Andy Goldsworthy.

3. Encourage students to come up with their own artistic uses for discarded, recycled, and natural materials and objects.

Reference

Stribling, M. L. 1970. *Art from found materials.* New York: Crown.

Resources

Barrentine, S. J. 1991. Once around the paper route. *Science and Children* 28 (1): 27–29.

Fioranelli, D. 2000. Recycling into art. *Science and Children* 38 (2): 30–33.

Gaylen, N. 1998. Encouraging curiosity at home. *Science and Children* 36 (4): 24–25.

Holly, K. 1998. The art of mathematics. *Teaching Children Mathematics* 4 (5): 266–267.

Lawrence, G. M. 1977. Project REUSE. *Science and Children* 14 (5): 25–27.

Sewall, S. B. 1991. The totem pole recycled. *Science and Children* 29 (5): 24–25.

White, O. L., and J. S. Townsend. 2008. Materials repurposed. *Science and Children* 45 (9): 36–39.

Ziemba, E. J., and J. Hoffman. 2006. Sorting and patterning in kindergarten. *Teaching Children Mathematics* 12 (5): 236–241.

+ Physical Science

Activity 8

Experimenting With Force and Motion Using Origami Frogs

Overview

Objects in motion and the forces that move them are the subjects of this lesson. This practical series of activities offers students a dynamic understanding of Newton's three laws of motion. In particular, the third law is investigated as students measure and analyze the jumping abilities of origami frogs.

Processes/Skills

- Observing
- Comparing
- Describing
- Making conclusions
- Experimenting
- Identifying patterns
- Predicting
- Constructing
- Measuring
- Applying
- Communicating
- Problem solving
- Developing spatial reasoning
- Inquiring
- Reflecting
- Creating
- Cooperating

Recommended For

Grades 3–4: Individual or small group instruction
You can adapt the lessons for grade 3 students by eliminating difficult vocabulary, such as *equilibrium* and *variable*; simplifying the math by omitting the graphing aspect of the lesson; and offering more assistance throughout the activity.

Time Required

2–3 hours

Materials Required for Main Activity

- Rubber ball
- Index card
- Cup or glass
- Quarter
- Spring
- Paper (various sizes and weights, including plenty of standard 8.5 in. × 11 in. photocopy paper)
- Student scissors
- Metersticks
- Calculators
- Graph paper

Materials Required for Going Further

- Various art supplies for decorating frogs (e.g., colored pencils, crayons, colored construction paper, glue sticks)

Connecting to the Standards

NSES
Grades K–4 Content Standards:
Standard A: Science as Inquiry

- Abilities necessary to do scientific inquiry (especially making good observations, planning and conducting a simple investigation, and communicating their ideas)

- Understanding about scientific inquiry (especially developing explanations using good evidence)

Standard B: Physical Science

- Properties of objects and materials (especially noticing the observable properties of objects and materials, and measuring those properties)

- Position and motion of objects (especially that an object's motion and position can be changed by pushing)

NCTM
Standards for Grades 3–5:

- Numbers and Operations (especially understanding and using numbers, operations, and estimation)

- Measurement (especially understanding units and processes of measurement and measurable aspects of objects)

- Reasoning and Proof (especially developing, selecting, and evaluating arguments and proofs)

- Communication (especially analyzing, organizing, and expressing their thinking clearly to peers and teachers)

Safety Considerations
Basic classroom safety practices apply.

Activity Objectives
In the following activity, students

- construct, test, and graphically compare the jumps made by three different sizes of frogs;

- predict how far a fourth frog would be expected to jump; and

- identify and test variables that affect frog-jumping ability.

Background Information
Newton's three laws of motion may be stated as follows:

- Law 1—Every object continues in its state of rest or of uniform motion, unless acted on by a force applied from the outside.

- Law 2—Change of motion is proportional to the applied force and takes place in the direction in which the force acts.

- Law 3—Whenever one object exerts a force on a second object, the second exerts an equal and opposite force on the first.

Write the three laws of motion on the chalkboard or on an overhead transparency so they are visible throughout this lesson.

Main Activity, Step-by-Step Procedures

1a. Engage the class by setting a rubber ball on a desk. Ask, "What forces are acting on the ball?" If students respond, "None," point out that gravity acts on the ball because it isn't floating away. Ask students, "If gravity is acting on the ball, why doesn't it fall to the ground?" (The desk stops it.) "Is the desk providing an upward force that counteracts the downward force of gravity?" (Yes.) Express this relationship on the chalkboard as a simple diagram (see Figure 8.1). Explain that the ball is not moving because the forces are in balance and that the ball is at rest or is in a state of equilibrium. Ask students, "Why does the ball stay at rest?" (Because the forces acting on it are in balance.) "Which of Newton's laws of motion do we see demonstrated here?" (Law 1, because the ball remains at rest.) Allow students time to work in groups to try to determine a response.

FIGURE 8.1.
Gravity pushes down. Desk pushes up.

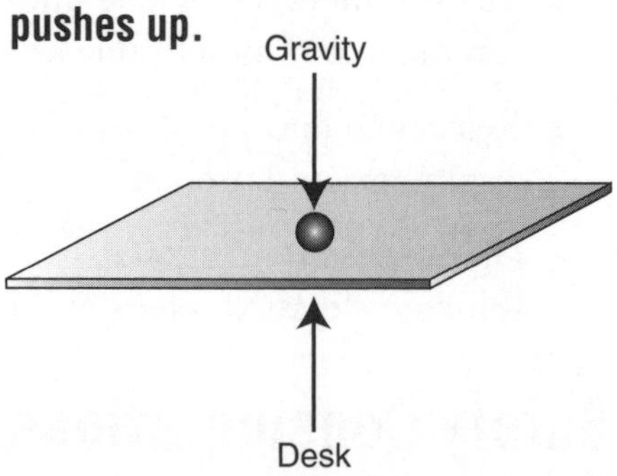

1b. Next, place an index card over an empty glass. Place a quarter on top of the card (see Figure 8.2). Ask students to predict what will happen to the quarter when you flick the card (in a horizontal direction parallel to the table top) away from the cup. Ask, "What could the quarter *possibly* do when I flick the card?" (It could go flying along with the card, for example, or it could fall into the cup; encourage divergent answers). Now, flick the card quickly. The quarter will fall straight down into the cup. Ask students to explain why this happened, giving them a few minutes in groups to work out an explanation. Ask, "What forces were acting on the quarter?" (Gravity pushes down and the card pushes up. When the card was removed, though, only gravity was acting on the quarter,

and it was forced to drop straight down.) You can let students try this themselves in their groups with a cup, an index card, and a quarter. Ask them, "Which of Newton's laws of motion do we see demonstrated in this activity?" (Laws 1 and 2, because the coin remained at rest until the card was quickly removed, allowing the force of gravity to act on it, pulling it down.) Again, allow students time to work in groups to try to determine a response.

FIGURE 8.2.
Quarter and index card on empty cup

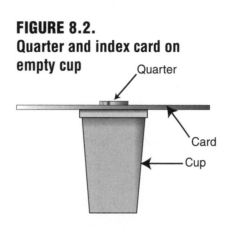

1c. Hold the rubber ball in your hand at about shoulder height. Ask students, "Which law(s) of motion are being demonstrated?" (Law 1, the ball continues in its state of rest.) Then ask, "What will happen to the ball if I let it go?" They will likely say it will fall. "Will anything else happen to the ball?" Wait for responses. Demonstrate by letting the ball go. "Which law(s) of motion does the falling ball demonstrate?" (Law 2, by releasing the ball we allowed gravity to act on it.) Are students getting the idea? Are you waiting a few seconds after asking your questions to allow more students to consider the information and to come up with answers? Now, bounce the rubber ball on the floor. Ask, "What forces are acting on the ball?" (The force of your throw and the force of gravity.) "Why does it bounce back?" (The falling ball exerts a force on the floor, but the floor also exerts a force back on the ball.) "Which of Newton's laws of motion do we see demonstrated in this activity?" Again, allow students time to work in groups to try to determine a response. (In the bouncing ball, we see a demonstration of all three laws of motion. The first law is demonstrated because the motionless ball is placed in motion by the forces acting on it—by the force of the throw and the force of gravity. The second law is demonstrated because the ball's motion is in the direction in which the forces— throwing and gravity—act, and is in proportion to the strength of those forces. The harder you throw, the more significant the change of motion of the ball. Newton's third law is also demonstrated, because the first object, the ball, exerts a force on a second object, the floor, which exerts an equal and opposite force on the first, shown by the ball bouncing back away from the floor.)

SCIENCE
Abilities necessary to do
   scientific inquiry
Position and motion of
   objects

MATH
Numbers and operations
Measurement

1d. You can also demonstrate Newton's third law by standing on a skateboard or on roller skates and pushing against a wall. As you push into the wall, you will roll back away from the wall (be careful not to fall!). You can even show this by just standing still and pushing on the wall, but it's more dramatic with the wheels underneath you. The third law is sometimes stated another way: For every action there is an equal and opposite reaction.

1e. Compress a spring against a desk or other flat surface and then release it, after asking students to predict what will happen. What did happen? Ask students to try to explain the spring's motion. "Are any of Newton's laws of motion at work here? What forces are acting on the spring?" (The spring demonstrates all laws, but especially Newton's third law of motion: As the spring pushes into the desk, the desk pushes back, sending the spring flying into the air, away from the desk.) This demonstration allows you to check for student comprehension before proceeding with the next activity.

2a. Show students an origami frog that you have constructed (see Figure 8.3). Explain that origami is the Japanese art of paper folding. To make the frog hop, press down sharply with your finger in the middle of its back at the edge, and let your finger slip off. This should provide the frog with a springing motion. Show students how the frog jumps, and they will be anxious to build their own.

2b. Let them work in groups, but have each student build his or her own jumping frog according to the diagram, using standard-size notebook or photocopy paper (8.5 in. × 11 in.—constructing the frog from a 217 mm, or 8.5 in., square). It might be easier to lead younger students through the folding process step-by-step. Give students some time just to play with their frogs, trying to make them jump well (high and far). Ask students to pay attention to specific techniques that make the frogs jump.

2c. Next, show students small- and medium-size frogs that you have constructed. Ask, "Which of these frogs do you think will jump the farthest? How could we find out?" Pass out copies of Activity Sheet 8.1 (p. 78) and have students complete the "Predictions" portion. Allow time for students to make two more frogs (from the same type of paper as the first), one from a square that is 63 mm wide, and another from a square that is 140 mm wide.

3. At this point, each student should have a "frog family"—a small, a medium, and a large frog. Students are now ready to test the frogs

for their distance-jumping abilities. Using metersticks and working in groups, they should record three good jumps per frog on Activity Sheet 8.1. Students can then calculate the average jump distance for each of the three frogs. More advanced students can also plot a graph of the frog jumps using the three averages (frog size on the x axis in millimeters, and jump length on the y axis in centimeters). Ask students, "How did your predictions stack up? Did frog size have an effect on jumping distance? Why or why not? Were you surprised by the outcome? Did the winning frog actually win every contest (if the contest is based on a single jump) or did it tend to win most of the contests (i.e., are the jumps consistent in their distances)? What did you learn from the frog-jumping activity? What does this activity have to do with Newton's laws of motion?" (The folded frog acts like a compressed spring—when released, it hops, demonstrating Newton's

SCIENCE
Understanding about scientific inquiry

MATH
Reasoning and proof
Communication

FIGURE 8.3. Constructing the origami frog

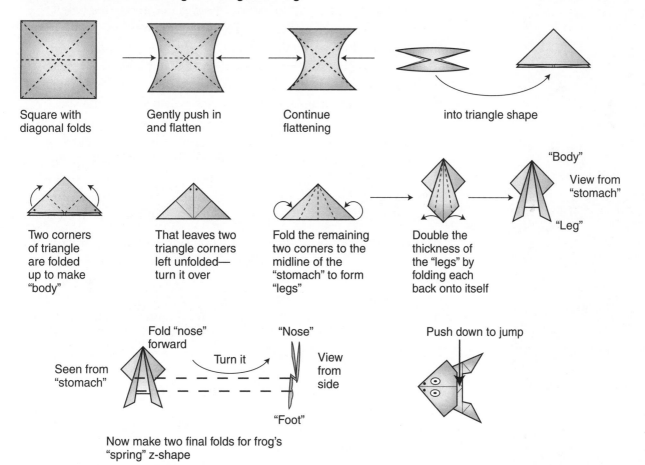

third law of motion.) Ask, "Based on the graph of the three average jump lengths, how far can a fourth frog (built from another 180 mm wide square of the same paper) be expected to jump?" Tell students to record their predictions, provide a rationale for those predictions (written or oral), build the fourth frog, and find out. Then ask students for an explanation of the results.

4. Introduce the concept of *variables*—aspects of the frog (such as its size), or characteristics of the frog's environment (such as the surface on which it is placed) that may be changed and that may have an effect on the frog's ability to jump. Ask the class to brainstorm all the variables they can think of that may have an effect on the frog's distance-jumping ability. These may include the frog's design, its size, the type of paper used, added weight such as a paper clip, the method of making it jump, and so on. Encourage divergent thinking here, even if you believe that the students' variables won't affect jumping ability (such as the color of the frog).

Next, instruct each group to choose one variable and to explore its effect on the distance-jumping ability of the origami frog. Students should do this by varying that chosen variable and recording the results. For instance, one group could make several different frogs each out of a different kind of paper. They would then record several jumps from each frog and calculate the averages, which should indicate which paper worked best. Be sure that students understand that only one variable is changed at a time, or else the results will be inconclusive. That is, if students vary the paper *and* the size at the same time, they won't know whether it was the paper or the size change that was responsible for any differences in jump length. If paper is the variable to be tested, all other variables (e.g., size, design) must be held constant.

Although this can be a slippery concept for elementary students, it is easiest for them to understand in relation to their own experiments. You can point out, in a concrete way, the need for changing only one variable at a time if you refer to the experiments and explorations that they are in the process of conducting. For example, as you circulate around the room and observe the group testing paper type, ask, "What would happen if you varied the size of the frog at the same time you varied the type of paper used?" Continue with this line of inquiry, as necessary, referring to students' own frogs. When their research is complete, each group can report its findings to the class. Ask them to explain their findings. For example, if paper type seemed to matter, why was it a factor?

Discussion Questions

Ask students the following:

1. How is the paper frog similar to a real frog? How is it different?

2. Which of Newton's laws of motion do you think you encounter most often in everyday life? Explain.

3. Can you think of any forms of transportation that use or demonstrate Newton's laws of motion? Can you think of any that do not?

4. Why do real frogs jump? Why would a real frog who can jump far or accurately have a survival advantage over frogs who can't jump as well? Think of as many reasons as you can.

Assessment

Suggestions for specific ways to assess student understanding are provided in parentheses.

1. Were students able to construct, test, and compare the jumps made by the three frogs in their frog families? (Use embedded observations during Procedures 3 and 4 as performance assessment.)

2. After test jumping their three frogs, were students able to predict how far a fourth frog would be expected to jump, based on their graph of the three average jump lengths? (Use observations of students during Procedure 3 as a performance assessment.)

3. Were students able to successfully identify and test variables that affected frog-jumping ability? (Use observations of students during Procedure 4 as a performance assessment.)

RUBRIC 8.1
Sample rubric using these assessment options

	Achievement Level		
	Developing 1	Proficient 2	Exemplary 3
Were students able to construct, test, and compare the jumps made by the three frogs in their frog families?	Constructed the frogs but had difficulty testing and comparing the results	Constructed, tested, and compared the frogs' jumps	Constructed, tested, and compared the frogs' jumps, and were able to discuss the process thoroughly
After testing their three frogs, were students able to predict how far a fourth frog would be expected to jump, based on their graph of the three average jump lengths?	Tried to predict the fourth frog's jump but were unable to do so	Predicted the fourth frog's jump, but were unable to discuss their understanding of the situation at length	Predicted the fourth frog's jump and were able to discuss their understanding of the situation at length

Going Further

Students can decorate their origami frogs in a number of ways at any point during the frog activities. Students can make beautiful frogs, scary frogs, camouflaged frogs (that live in a rain forest or a desert pond), happy frogs, confident frogs, or shy frogs. Encourage divergent and creative thinking. Ask students, "Some frogs are poisonous (e.g., poison arrow frogs, genus *Dendrobates*, from tropical Central and South America). If the frogs want predators to know that they are dangerous, should they be dull or brightly colored?" (See if students can find a picture of a poison arrow frog to check their predictions—they are very brightly colored to alert potential predators.) Ask each student to decorate a frog for life in a specific habitat (such as a rain forest; a large or mountain lake; a desert, small, or weedy pond; or a tree) and to explain in a journal writing assignment why the frog looks as it does. Students can show and tell about their decorated frogs. Encourage divergent and innovative thinking.

Other Options and Extensions

Challenge the class to use what they know about distance jumping to produce the longest-jumping frog possible. Hold a class competition to see which group can build the longest-jumping frog. Have several different sorts of paper, paper clips, brads, and so forth on hand, as well as plenty of tools (e.g., rulers, metersticks, paper punches, compasses). Ask, "Was the winning frog the one you would have predicted as the best jumper? Why or why not?"

Hold other sorts of frog-jumping competitions. Hold contests to determine which frog jumps the highest, with the most accuracy (from lily pad *A*

to lily pad *B*), which frog is the biggest or smallest, and so on. If you opt to eschew classroom competition in favor of a cooperative effort, each student group could explore a different aspect of frog hopping, after which the class could demonstrate and discuss frog abilities in a "frog-hopping exposition."

Have students read "The Notorious Jumping Frog of Calaveras County" by Mark Twain (1993).

Reference

Twain, M. 1993. The notorious jumping frog of Calaveras county. In *The Harper American literature, vol. 2*, eds. Donald McQuade et al., 269–272. New York: Harper Collins.

Resources

Adams, B. 2007. Energy in motion. *Science and Children* 44 (7): 58–60.

Ashbrook, P. 2008. Objects in motion. *Science and Children* 45 (7): 14–16.

Dana, T. M., R. Perkins, K. Ledford, and M. St. Pierre. 1993. Fun-filled physics. *Science and Children* 30 (7): 28–31.

Meyer, K. J. 1993. Folding frogs. *Science and Children* 30 (5): 12–14.

Robertson, W. C., J. Gallagher, and W. Miller. 2004. Newton's first law: Not so simple after all. *Science and Children* 41 (6): 25–29.

Toll, D., and S. Stump. 2007. Characteristics of shapes. *Teaching Children Mathematics* 13 (9): 472–473.

Turner, E. E., D. L. Junk, and S. B. Empson. 2007. The power of paper-folding tasks. *Teaching Children Mathematics* 13 (6): 322–329.

ACTIVITY SHEET 8.1
Experimenting With Force and Motion Using Origami Frogs

Prediction

1. Which frog will jump the farthest, on average? (Circle one)

Large frog   Medium frog   Small frog

Why do you think so?

2. Which frog will jump the farthest, on average? (Circle one)

Large frog   Medium frog   Small frog

Why do you think so?

3. Data Collection

Frog	Frog Width (mm)	Frog Length (mm)	Jump Distance #1 (cm)	Jump Distance #2 (cm)	Jump Distance #3 (cm)	Average Jump Distance (cm)
Large						
Medium						
Small						

Analysis

4. Were your predictions accurate? Why or why not?

5. Was the frog with the largest average jump distance also the frog that had the single longest jump? How do you explain this?

6. Graph your data, with frog length on the *x* axis and average jump length for each frog on the *y* axis.

Conclusions

7. Based on your experiment, data, and analysis, what have you learned about the jumping origami frogs? Does frog size have an effect on jumping ability? How do you know?

Further Study

8. What other factors can you think of that will affect an origami frog's jumping ability?

9. Based on your graph, how far can a fourth frog (built from a 180 mm wide square of the same paper) be expected to jump? (Be sure to record your procedure, data, and results below.)

Physical Science

Activity 9

What Makes a Boat Float?

Overview

Whether or not a boat floats is determined by its shape and density. In this activity, students discover how and why boats float by designing different hull shapes and finding which design holds the most weight. Students record, calculate, and interpret data as they learn about buoyancy in this hands-on activity.

Processes/Skills

- Observing
- Problem solving
- Predicting
- Describing
- Analyzing
- Concluding
- Measuring
- Calculating
- Inquiring
- Communicating
- Recognizing shapes and patterns
- Developing spatial sense
- Cooperating

Recommended For

Grades 3–4: Small group instruction
The lesson can be simplified for students in grades K–2 by using only one or two pieces of foil, offering more boat shape ideas, simplifying the vocabulary

appropriately, and minimizing the math involved. Younger students can still make predictions and design and test boats, and with your help they can create a bar graph of shape versus pennies held. Another option would be to conduct the activity for younger students as a teacher-led demonstration.

Time Required

1–3 hours

Materials Required for Main Activity

- Modeling clay
- Aluminum foil
- Small tubs of water
- Small weights (pennies, metric weights, metal washers, or any small, standardized objects)
- Metric rulers
- Calculators
- Graph paper

Connecting to the Standards

NSES
Grades K–4 Content Standards:

Standard B: Physical Science

- Properties of objects and materials (especially noticing the observable properties of objects and materials, and measuring those properties)

Standard E: Science and Technology

- Abilities of technological design (especially proposing, implementing, and evaluating a solution to a technological problem)
- Understanding about science and technology (especially that investigators can work together to solve problems)

NCTM
Standards for Grades PreK–2, 3–5:

- Numbers and Operations (especially understanding and using numbers, operations, and estimation)

- Geometry (especially identifying, naming, and/or comparing two- and three-dimensional shapes)

- Problem Solving (especially constructing new math knowledge through problem solving)

- Connections (especially noting the valuable interconnections between mathematics and science)

- Representation (especially using representation to record and communicate mathematical ideas and to solve problems)

Safety Considerations

Basic classroom safety practices apply.

Activity Objectives

In the following activity, students

- design and build boats to carry loads and explain why some designs worked better than others; and

- explain why a boat floats, using their own data and the concepts of displacement, density, mass, and volume.

Background Information

Two factors, density and shape, determine whether an object floats or sinks. Density is the relative weight of an object, defined mathematically as the object's mass divided by volume. A more dense object or material has more tightly packed internal particles. A brick, for instance, is more dense (that is, it has more tightly packed particles within it) than a piece of wood (which has more loosely packed particles). A brick is more dense than water, and it will sink. Most wood, however, is less dense than water, allowing it to float. Therefore, it is not an object's weight alone that determines whether it will sink or float: It is the object's weight (really its mass) divided by its volume. A really large piece of Styrofoam (say, 500 kg) will float in water despite its large mass because it is less dense than the water. That is, it has less mass per unit of volume than water. Put another way, if we have two equal volumes (say, 250 cm^3) of Styrofoam and of water, the Styrofoam is lighter in weight (or contains less mass). The Styrofoam is less dense than the water and therefore it will float. Density is related to buoyancy, which can be thought of as the tendency of an object to float in a liquid, or as the upthrust that the liquid exerts on an object floating within it. Dense materials are not very buoyant, and buoyant materials are not very dense.

WHAT MAKES A BOAT FLOAT?

The other factor that determines floating or sinking is shape. The shape of an object, like a boat, allows it to push water out of the way, which is referred to as displacement of the water. If a boat, and the air contained in it, displaces more water than the weight of the boat itself, it floats. Large boats and heavy boats, therefore, must displace a great deal of water. If the boat displaces less water than the weight of the boat itself, it sinks. The shape of the boat, then, is crucial in determining how much weight the boat can carry and whether the boat floats (as demonstrated in the following activity). You could say that a boat's shape strongly influences its buoyancy or that a boat's buoyancy is determined by that boat's density and shape.

Main Activity, Step-by-Step Procedures

1. Begin by showing students a small, flattened piece of modeling clay. Bend it into a very roughly shaped boat. Ask students, "Will it float?" Then place the clay into a small tub of water (5–10 cm deep). The clay floats. Next, mold the clay into a tight ball. Ask students, "Will the ball float (after all, it's the same clay)?" Once again, place the clay in the water. This time, the clay sinks. Ask students to conclude what they can about floating and sinking in this situation. Give them a moment in groups to discuss and then listen to their ideas. Obviously the shape matters. Ask students, "Does the boat's size matter?" Demonstrate that the clay can be doubled or tripled in size but will still float if shaped like a boat and will sink if shaped like a ball. The boat's shape matters more than its size.

2. Now try an exercise to challenge your students. Provide each student group with three 15 cm × 15 cm pieces of aluminum foil, a pile of pennies, and a small tub of water (you can substitute metric weights, metal washers, or any small, standardized objects for the pennies). Challenge students to design a boat that can float as many pennies as possible (they can shape their boats any way they choose). Each boat has to float with its load of pennies for at least 5 seconds for the trial to count. Encourage students to brainstorm before beginning the activity: What boat shapes are possible? Students must try at least three different boat shapes, predicting how many pennies each will hold before loading the boat with pennies. Then each group runs three trials with each of the three boats and records data in a table (see Activity Sheet 9.1, p. 86). In the table students briefly describe each of three boat shapes that they tried (younger students could draw a picture of the boats rather than describe them in words), list how many pennies each shape held in each trial, and average the

SCIENCE
Properties of objects and
  materials
Abilities of technological
  design
Understanding about
  science and technology

MATH
Geometry
Problem solving

MATH
Numbers and operations
Communication
Representation

trials for each boat. Finally, groups record and discuss their conclusions. Younger students can generate a bar graph, with teacher help, of the number of pennies held for each basic boat shape.

3. In the next exercise, older and more advanced student groups discover whether the area of the base of the boat is related to the number of pennies that it can hold. Using three more 15 cm × 15 cm sheets of foil, groups perform three trials with each of the three boat designs again (designs should include low, flat boats and tall, slim boats), this time recording the approximate area of boat base (i.e., the bottom of the hull) versus the maximum number of pennies held in each trial. Hull area can be determined using metric rulers, calculators, and area formulas (remind students that the surface area is πr^2 for generally circular hulls, and length times width for generally rectangular hulls). Predictions and data can be recorded on Activity Sheet 9.1. Students can then graph the area of the base of each boat (x axis) versus the average number of pennies that it held (y axis). Students should look for patterns in the data and the graph, and document their conclusions. (Generally, the wider the hull, the more weight the boat can handle without sinking because the load is spread over a wider area.)

4. Finally, host an open competition for the boat design that can hold the greatest number of pennies. Student groups design and construct their best boat, using what they've learned in the lesson so far. Test all boats in a classwide demonstration to determine the winner. Students can then write their observations, thoughts, reactions, conclusions, and questions in their science journals.

Discussion Questions

Ask students the following:

1. With your boat, did the height of the sides matter? Why? In a real boat, would the height of the sides matter? Why? What kinds of boats have wide flat bottoms (or hulls)? What are they generally used for? What kinds of boats have small, knifelike hulls? What are they generally used for?

2. Describe the sort of boat you would want if you were hauling heavy loads of ore on a river. Describe the design you would want if you were trying to race other boats.

3. Of the two factors determining floating/sinking (density and shape), which do you think is more important to boat design, and why?

MATH
Problem solving

WHAT MAKES A BOAT FLOAT?

Assessment

Suggestions for specific ways to assess student understanding are provided in parentheses.

1. Were students able to design and build boats that supported loads, and could they explain, based on their own data, why certain hull designs worked better than others? (Use embedded observations during Procedures 3 and 4 as performance assessments, and use Discussion Question 3 as a prompt for a science journal entry.)

2. Could students explain why a wider hull generally holds more weight and how they determined an answer to that question? (Listen carefully to student responses to Discussion Question 2 as an embedded assessment or as a prompt for a science journal entry.)

3. Were students able to explain how a boat floats, using their own data and the concepts of displacement, density, mass, and volume? (Pay attention to their activity and discussion during Procedures 2–4 as performance assessment and embedded evidence.)

RUBRIC 9.1
Sample rubric using these assessment options

	Achievement Level		
	Developing 1	Proficient 2	Exemplary 3
Were students able to design and build boats that supported loads, and could they explain, based on their own data, why certain hull designs worked better than others?	Attempted to build load-carrying boats, and did so with some success, but were unable to explain why some designs worked better than others	Successfully built several load-carrying boats and could explain why some of their boats worked better than others	Successfully built several load-carrying boats and could explain why some of their own boats, as well as the boats of other students, worked better than others
Could students explain why a wider hull generally holds more weight and how they determined an answer to that question?	Attempted to explain but were unable to do so effectively	Successfully explained the effectiveness of a wide hull but did not apply math concepts or terminology to do so	Successfully explained the effectiveness of a wide hull, and did so by using their own data as well as math concepts and terminology
Were students able to explain how a boat floats, using their own data and the concepts of displacement, density, mass, and volume?	Attempted to explain but were unable to do so effectively	Successfully explained flotation using science concepts but did not apply math concepts or terminology	Successfully explained flotation using science concepts, as well as math concepts and terminology

Other Options and Extensions

Tell students to research boat design using the library or the internet. Ask them, "Do any of the boats you found look like boats that you designed? Explain."

Ask students, "What are some things, other than boats, that float? What makes those objects float?"

Resources

Adams, B. 2006. London Bridge is falling down. *Science and Children* 43 (8): 49–51.

Bloom, S. J. 1994. Data buddies: Primary grade mathematicians explore. *Teaching Children Mathematics* 1 (1): 80–86.

Martin, S., J. Sharp, and L. Zachary. 2004. Thinking engineering. *Science and Children* 41 (4): 18–23.

Saltonstall, S. 1986. Ship shape. *Science and Children* 24 (1): 48–49.

Scheckel, L. 1993. How to make density float. *Science and Children* 31 (3): 30–33.

Schomburg, A. 2008. The better boat challenge. *Science and Children* 46 (2): 36–39.

WHAT MAKES A BOAT FLOAT?

ACTIVITY SHEET 9.1
What Makes a Boat Float?

1. Prediction: Which boat shape will hold the most pennies? Why?

	Boat 1	Boat 2	Boat 3
Describe the boat's shape			
Prediction: number of pennies boat will hold			
Pennies held, Trial 1			
Pennies held, Trial 2			
Pennies held, Trial 3			
Average number of pennies held			

Conclusions:

2. Prediction: Which boat shape will hold the most pennies? Why?

	Boat 1	Boat 2	Boat 3
Approximate area of hull base (cm²)			
Prediction: number of pennies boat will hold			
Pennies held, Trial 1			
Pennies held, Trial 2			
Pennies held, Trial 3			
Average number of pennies held			

On a separate piece of paper or the back of this sheet, graph the average pennies for each boat versus the approximate area of that boat's hull.

Conclusions:

Physical Science

Activity 10
Investigating the Properties of Magnets

Overview

In this activity, younger students encounter, discuss, and apply the basic characteristics of magnets and magnetism as they explore and elaborate on their experiences. Student groups implement some of the terminology and concepts appropriate to the study of magnets as they investigate and measure how far magnets can repel one another and how many paper clips their magnets can attract.

Processes/Skills

- Observing
- Connecting
- Describing
- Analyzing
- Concluding
- Measuring
- Calculating
- Problem solving
- Communicating
- Cooperating

Recommended For

Grades K–4: Small group instruction
Offer students in grades K–1 extra assistance during the exploration in Procedure 1, and simplify the introduced vocabulary as necessary. You can also simplify the quantitative "repel" and "attract" investigations in Procedure 3 or even conduct those activities as teacher-led demonstrations.

Time Required

1–2 hours

Materials Required for Main Activity

- An assortment of shapes and sizes of small magnets (available through science supply catalogues, electronics stores, toy stores, and dollar stores)
- An assortment of miscellaneous objects and materials (such as paper clips, index cards, plastic pen caps)
- String
- Paper clips
- Metersticks or metric rulers

Connecting to the Standards

NSES
Grades K–4 Content Standards:

Standard A: Science as Inquiry

- Abilities necessary to do scientific inquiry (especially making good observations, planning and conducting a simple investigation, and communicating their ideas)
- Understanding about scientific inquiry (especially developing explanations using good evidence)

Standard B: Physical Science

- Light, heat, electricity, and magnetism (especially that magnets attract and repel one another and other materials)

NCTM
Standards for Grades PreK–2, 3–5:

- Measurement (especially understanding units and processes of measurement and measurable aspects of objects)
- Problem Solving (especially constructing new math knowledge through problem solving)
- Reasoning and Proof (especially developing, selecting, and evaluating arguments and proofs)

Safety Considerations

Basic classroom safety practices apply. Caution students that opposing magnets must not become flying projectiles as the magnets repel one another. Batteries used to make electromagnets (in Other Options and Extensions) should be used only under adult supervision.

Activity Objectives

In the following activity, students

- actively explore magnets and their interactions; and

- determine, via quantitative and qualitative inquiry, whether magnetism is cumulative.

Main Activity, Step-by-Step Procedures

1. Begin the lesson with an open exploration of the magnets. Present student groups with some concrete materials (several magnets of varying shapes and sizes and a few miscellaneous objects such as paper clips, index cards, plastic pen caps), little or no introduction or direction by the teacher, and ample time to "play" with the materials. Simply give the groups time to do some trial-and-error exploration with the materials, under the condition that when the agreed upon time is up (15 minutes should be sufficient), each group will briefly report to the class regarding something that they learned about the materials and how they interact. (One student should be chosen to keep brief notes and drawings of the findings.) During the exploration time, circulate among the groups, gently facilitating an inquiry of the materials' interactions but not pressing students in any particular direction; encourage divergent and innovative thinking.

2. When the exploration time is up, allow each group to choose a spokesperson who reports one aspect of what the group members learned to the class (usually the person who took the notes and made drawings of the findings). As students talk about their findings, reinforce or introduce appropriate terms and concepts through nurturing and inquisitive dialogue. Depending on the grade level, such terms might include, but would not be limited to, *push, pull, attraction, repulsion, poles, attract,* and *repel.* Concepts and terms may be reinforced or introduced through comments and questions. For example, "I notice that you said the magnets 'stuck together'—in science we might say that they were *attracted* to each other." Or,

SCIENCE
Abilities necessary to do scientific inquiry

SCIENCE
Understanding about scientific inquiry

MATH
Measurement
Problem solving
Reasoning and proof

"You mentioned that the magnets could push away from each other, even through the index card. That's a very good observation. We could say that the magnets push or *repel* each other. Can the magnets do this no matter how they are arranged?" The point is for students to have an opportunity to use authentic dialogue when connecting science ideas to their own exploratory experiences.

**FIGURE 10.1.
Magnet and
paper clips**

Magnet

3. Student groups can elaborate on their understanding by measuring how far one magnet can push another magnet of similar size and shape (instruct students to hold the magnets together and let one "spring" away in repulsion from the first). After predicting the number, students conduct five trials and record the data in Activity Sheet 10.1, Table 10.1 (p. 94; for older students, average the trials). Next, students measure and record how far two magnets can push a single magnet (Table 10.2). Then students try it with three magnets pushing a single magnet (Table 10.3). Graph the class results (number of magnets pushing versus distance pushed). Compare results and reach conclusions together as a class. Ask students, "Is 'magnet power' cumulative?"

4. Next, have each group tie or tape a magnet to a string and tape the other end of the string to the edge of a desk so that the magnet hangs freely in the air. Students then predict how many paper clips the magnet can attract and hold (Table 10.4). To determine exactly how many paper clips the magnet can hold, students run three trials, record and average the data, and reach conclusions. After students are done with their trials, ask them to place the paper clips end-to-end so that the clips are just touching, but not hooked together (see Figure 10.1). Ask students, "How many paper clips can the magnet hold now? How do you explain the fact that the paper clips can attract other paper clips? Can paper clips do this when they are not touching a magnet?" Then say, "You saw how many paper clips could be held up by a single magnet. Next, predict how many clips can be held by two magnets tied together."

Another option is to have each student group discuss, invent, illustrate, and report to the class on (though not necessarily build) an invention that uses magnets and/or magnetism.

5. Finally, find out what else the students want to know about magnets. Especially for older students, allow them to measure something else about magnets—something that they devise and want to know about, such as how much mass a particular magnet can lift or whether differently shaped magnets can lift different amounts of material. The groups should carry out and eventually report on their investigations.

Discussion Questions

Ask students the following:

1. What have you learned about magnets and magnetism? What did you do to find this out?

2. What do you still want to know about magnets and magnetism? How could you find out what you want to know?

3. How can magnets and magnetism be useful to us in everyday life?

4. When we measured how far one magnet would "spring away" from the other (Procedure 3), why did we conduct five trials and then calculate an average rather than just doing a single trial?

Assessment

Suggestions for specific ways to assess student understanding are provided in parentheses.

1. Did students actively explore magnets and their interactions? (Use your observations of student activity during Procedure 1 as an embedded assessment.)

2. Were students successful in connecting meaningful science terms and concepts to their exploratory experiences, and in applying those concepts and terms to their expanded investigations? (Listen to student responses to Discussion Questions 1–3 during Procedures 1–5 as embedded evidence, or use the Discussion Questions as prompts for science journal entries.)

3. Were students able, via quantitative and qualitative inquiry, to determine whether magnetism is cumulative? (Use student responses to the exercises in Activity Sheet 10.1 as a form of performance assessment.)

RUBRIC 10.1
Sample rubric using these assessment options

	Achievement Level		
	Developing 1	Proficient 2	Exemplary 3
Did students actively explore magnets and their interactions?	Marginally engaged in the exploration process	Satisfactorily engaged in the exploration process	Significantly engaged in the exploration process
Were students successful in connecting meaningful science terms and concepts to their exploratory experiences, and in applying those concepts and terms to their expanded investigations?	Some success with discussing terms and concepts but unable to connect or apply them to any significant extent	Satisfactory success with connecting the terms to their experiences and some success in applying them to their expanded investigations	Significant success connecting the terms to their experiences and in applying them to their expanded investigations
Were students able, via quantitative and qualitative inquiry, to determine whether magnetism is cumulative?	Attempted the investigations, but unable to clearly determine	Able to clearly determine	Able to clearly determine and applied that understanding in discussions relating to their earlier explorations and findings with magnets

Other Options and Extensions

1. Challenge students to figure out how an electromagnet works and ask them to make one from a battery and a length of insulated wire.

2. Ask students to figure out how an electric motor works. Ask them, "What do magnets have to do with it? Can you build an electric motor of your own?"

3. Ask students, "What does magnetism have to do with generating electricity? Can you find out how a generator works?"

Resources

Ashbrook, P. 2005. More than messing around with magnets. *Science and Children* 43 (2): 21–23.

Burns, J. C., and C. Buzzelli. 1992. An active attraction. *Science and Children* 30 (1): 20–22.

McCartney, R.W., S. Deroche, and D. Pontiff. 2008. Can trains really float? *Science and Children* 45 (7): 33–37.

Milson, J. L. 1990. Electromagnetic attraction. *Science and Children* 28 (1): 24–25.

Orozco, G. T., P. S. Alberu, and E. R. Haynes. 1994. The electromagnetic swing. *Science and Children* 31 (6): 20–21.

Sharp, J. 1996. Manipulatives for the metal chalkboard. *Teaching Children Mathematics* 2 (5): 280–281.

Teachworth, M. D. 1991. A memory for magnets. *Science and Children* 29 (2): 30–31.

Whiten, D. J., and P. Whiten. 2003. Talk counts: Discussing graphs with young children. *Teaching Children Mathematics* 10 (3): 142–149.

93

ACTIVITY SHEET 10.1
Investigating the Properties of Magnets

1. How far can *one* magnet "push" another magnet (from Procedure 3)?

    (Prediction: _____ cm)

TABLE 10.1

Trial	Distance (cm)
1	
2	
3	
4	
5	
Average	

2. How far can *two* magnets "push" another magnet (from Procedure 3)?

    (Prediction: _____ cm)

TABLE 10.2

Trial	Distance (cm)
1	
2	
3	
4	
5	
Average	

3. How far can *three* magnets "push" another magnet (from Procedure 3)?

(Prediction: _____ cm)

TABLE 10.3

Trial	Distance (cm)
1	
2	
3	
4	
5	
Average	

Conclusions:

4. How many paper clips can the hanging magnet attract at one time (from Procedure 4)?

(Prediction: _____ clips)

TABLE 10.4

Trial	Number of paper clips
1	
2	
3	
Average	

Conclusions:

Chemical Science

Activity 11

Applying Simple Chromatography

Overview

This activity involves chemistry, mystery, colors, and measurement. Students observe the composition of various inks by separating them via water-based chromatography. Students use what they learn about chromatography to solve a mystery involving a suspicious note and five different marking pens. Working together, they devise a plan to find out who wrote the note—a great introduction to color mixing.

Processes/Skills

- Observing
- Measuring
- Predicting
- Describing
- Inferring
- Experimenting
- Communicating
- Estimating
- Comparing
- Reflecting
- Recognizing patterns
- Problem solving
- Creating
- Cooperating

APPLYING SIMPLE CHROMATOGRAPHY

Recommended For

Grades 3–4: Small group instruction
You can accomodate grade 3 students by simplifying the vocabulary, eliminating Procedure 3, and presenting the activity as a teacher-led demonstration.

Time Required

1–2 hours

Materials Required for Main Activity

- Paper towels
- A variety of water-soluble markers, inks, and paints
- Shallow plastic plates or saucers
- Empty two-liter plastic soda bottles

Materials Required for Going Further

- All of the materials required for the Main Activity
- An assortment of paper types
- Various drawing and painting materials

Connecting to the Standards

NSES
Grades K–4 Content Standards:
Standard A: Science as Inquiry

- Abilities necessary to do scientific inquiry (especially making good observations, planning and conducting a simple investigation, and communicating their ideas)
- Understanding about scientific inquiry (especially developing explanations using good evidence)

Standard B: Physical Science

- Properties of objects and materials (especially noticing the observable properties of objects and materials)

NCTM
Standards for Grades PreK–2, 3–5:

- Measurement (especially understanding units and processes of measurement and measurable aspects of objects)

- Problem Solving (especially constructing new math knowledge through problem solving)

Safety Considerations
Basic classroom safety practices apply.

Activity Objectives
In the following activity, students

- carry out several chromatographies;

- recognize and explain that some colors are actually mixtures of constituent colors;

- use chromatographic techniques to solve the "mystery pen" problem; and

- estimate and measure the ink's "rate of climb" during the chromatography process.

Background Information
Chromatography is a technique used by scientists to separate mixtures of pigments or other substances. It usually involves filter paper and solvents such as acetone, ether, or ethanol—chemicals that are unsuitable for elementary-level activities. For this activity, water, rather than potentially hazardous chemicals, is used to demonstrate the fundamentals of chromatography. The term *chromatography* is derived from the Greek *chroma*, which means "color," and *graphien*, which means "written or visual representation."

In these activities your students perform simple chromatography with various types and colors of water-soluble inks. *Water soluble* means that the inks dissolve, or go into solution, in the water. The inks should separate as they rise through the filter paper (i.e., paper towel), allowing students to observe the inks' constituent colors. Why does the water rise (against the force of gravity) into the paper towel, and why does the ink sometimes separate into other colors? The attraction of the water molecules to the fibers of the towel is stronger than the force of gravity acting on the water. The water is therefore absorbed by the towel (the same force that creates

APPLYING SIMPLE CHROMATOGRAPHY

STANDARDS

surface tension; see Activity 12, p. 107). When the water reaches the ink spot, the water-soluble ink pigment dissolves. The water and pigment molecules continue to rise together, based on their attraction to the towel fibers. Many colors of ink or paint are actually combinations of more than one color (as you will see when you perform the chromatography). As the

FIGURE 11.1. Initial setup

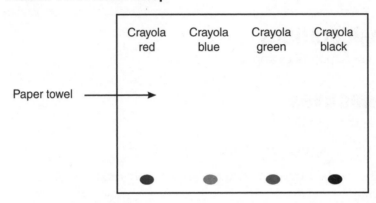

water and dissolved pigments rise, the heavier weight pigments settle first (lower in the towel), and the lighter weight pigments continue to rise, leaving a colorful pattern on the towel. Different black inks are composed of different color combinations, so each brand of ink can be identified by its distinguishing chromatography color pattern.

Main Activity, Step-by-Step Procedures

1. The first phase of this lesson is taught as a guided discovery experience. Begin by asking students what they know about colors. Can they identify colors just by looking (you might hold up a few different colored pens or other objects to make the point)? Ask students, "Can colors be combined into other colors? Can colors be separated into other colors?" Provide each student group (three to five students per group) with a paper towel and several colors of water-soluble markers. Have them make a 0.5 cm dot with each marker along the long edge of the towel (about 1 cm from the edge), marking in pencil the pen type and color used along the opposite long edge (see Figure 11.1). Tape the paper towel around a two-liter plastic soda bottle with the ink spots at the base of the bottle. Place the bottle and towel into a shallow plate or saucer of water (less than 1 cm deep) so that the paper towel just makes contact with the water, as in Figure 11.2. What do students observe? One of the group members should record

SCIENCE
Abilities necessary to do
  scientific inquiry
Understanding about
  scientific inquiry
Properties of objects and
  materials

MATH
Problem solving

their observations. Students should see that the water begins to "climb up" the towel, taking with it the ink from the spots. Have students time the ink's climb up the towel, record observations, and observe intermittently for an hour or so. Then ask students to remove the towel from the bottle (let it dry overnight if your schedule allows) and study the chromatogram that has been produced. Ask students, "Are the colors that climb the same colors as the original ink spots?" (It depends on the ink and the color used. Some will separate into a variety of colors, indicating their composition.) "Which colors separated? Which colors did not separate? Which colors are actually made up of other colors? Were you surprised by any of your results?" Have students measure the length of the various shades generated from each spot and compare the patterns produced. Ask students, "How do the chromatography patterns from the various colors, or the various brands or types of pens, compare? How do you explain the results?" Have each group report its results and explanations. Ask each group what they learned from this exploration.

FIGURE 11.2.
Towel taped to bottle

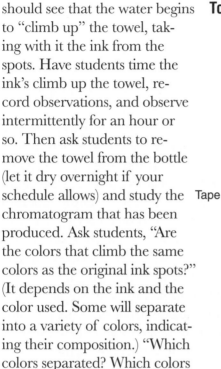
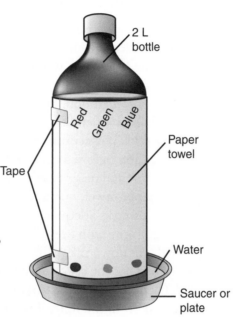

MATH
Measurement

2. Present the student groups with a problem to solve. Explain that in this hypothetical situation, five different people wrote notes in black ink on paper towels, but you don't know who wrote which note. You do know that each of the five people is known to write with a particular type of pen. Here are the pens that they use:

Person 1: Pentech Fineline Washable Marker

Person 2: Pilot G2 Gel Ink Pen

Person 3: Crayola Washable Marker, Classic Colors

Person 4: Sanford Calligraphic Water Based Ink Pen

Person 5: Rose Art Classic Washable Marker

APPLYING SIMPLE CHROMATOGRAPHY

(Each of these pens has a different type of black ink; you can certainly use others, but test the pen out first to see that the ink separates and that each chromatogram is readily distinguishable.)

The challenge here is to identify the writer of each note. Provide each student group with access to the five types of pens and a towel with the brief note written along the lower edge. Prepare the notes ahead of time, each written in a single type of ink. Be sure to keep track of which note has which ink by numbering the towels and keeping a hidden list of which ink was used on which towel (see Figure 11.3). Recommend that the groups discuss their plans of investigation before setting out. You can coach and gently guide their experimental designs as necessary. Set up five chromatograms on one paper towel, one for each of the known inks (be sure to separate the ink marks adequately, and label each ink using a pencil because the graphite won't separate when wet), and a sixth chromatogram of the uknown ink, which is already on its own paper towel. By performing the six chromatographies, students should be able to determine the chromatographic pattern of each ink type and of the ink from the note. They can then compare the patterns of the known and unknown inks to identify the note's writer.

FIGURE 11.3. Mystery setup

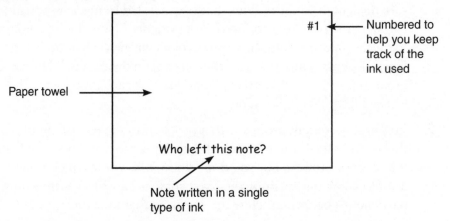

3. Ask students to estimate how long it takes for the ink colors to separate on the chromatography towel. Ask them how they know. Then ask how they could actually measure the time needed for the water and ink to rise in the paper. Will the different inks vary in terms of time needed to separate? One possible method to time

FIGURE 11.4. Rate setup

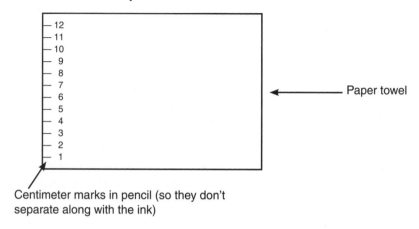

Paper towel

Centimeter marks in pencil (so they don't
separate along with the ink)

the ink separation is to prepare a paper towel with pencil marks at
each centimeter along the short side (see Figure 11.4). Then have
each group perform a chromatography on a particular ink and time
the rise of the ink and water in the towel in cm/minute, resulting
in a measurement of "rate of climb." Ask students, "What do you
predict will happen? Will the inks rise at different rates?"

Discussion Questions
Ask students the following:

1. What did you think would happen to the ink/paint spot on the towel?
    What did you think would happen to the water in the saucer?

2. What happened to the ink/paint spots on the paper towel? Can you
    explain how and why the colors separated?

3. Why do you suppose some colors separated and others did not?

4. Was it easy to tell the various pens apart, based on the way their col-
    ors separated during chromatography? Can you think of any ways
    that chromatography could be helpful to people in various jobs?

5. Was rate of climb an effective way to compare types of pens/inks/
    paints? Why or why not? What procedure did you use to measure
    rate of climb? How accurate was your estimate of the time it took
    for the colors to separate?

APPLYING SIMPLE CHROMATOGRAPHY

Assessment

Suggestions for specific ways to assess student understanding are provided in parentheses.

1. Were students able to successfully perform the chromatographies? (Use embedded observations during Procedures 1 and 2 as performance assessment.)

2. Did students recognize that some colors are actually made up of other constituent colors? (Listen to student responses to Discussion Questions 1–3 during Procedures 1 and 2 as embedded evidence, and use the Discussion Questions as prompts for science journal entries.)

3. Were students able to solve the mystery pen problem by comparing chromatography results? Were they able to explain their methods of investigation? (Use embedded observations and student responses to Discussion Question 4 during Procedures 1 and 2 as performance assessment, and use Discussion Question 4 as a prompt for science journal entries.)

RUBRIC 11.1
Sample rubric using these assessment options

| | Achievement Level | | |
	Developing 1	Proficient 2	Exemplary 3
Were students able to successfully perform the chromatographies?	Attempted but unsuccessfully	Succeeded satisfactorily	Succeeded satisfactorily and were able to clearly discuss the experience
Did students recognize that some colors are actually made up of other constituent colors?	Attempted to explain the constitution of the colors but were unable to do so to any significant extent	Clearly explained, using their chromatographic evidence, that some colored inks are made up of other colors	Clearly explained, using their chromatographic evidence, and also explained how the color separation takes place
Were students able to solve the mystery pen problem by comparing chromatography results? Were they able to explain their methods of investigation?	Attempted the investigation and explanation but were not successful on either	Solved the problem and explained generally their methods of investigation	Solved the problem and explained their methods of investigation, and also explained the place and value of such problem solving in science and mathematics
Were students able to estimate the time it would take for the colors to separate and to accurately measure the ink's rate of climb in the towel?	Estimated the time needed, but only roughly and with little or no explanation	Estimated and measured accurately	Estimated and measured accurately, and were able to explain the process taking place in the chromatogram

4. Were students able to estimate the time it would take for the colors to separate and to accurately measure the ink's rate of climb in the towel? (Use embedded observations during Procedure 3 as performance assessment.)

Going Further

Have students work in groups or on their own to create pictures using chromatography. Tell students to use a variety of inks, paints, and dyes on different types of paper. Once the paper dries, students can add lines or drawings as they wish. Encourage experimentation and innovation. Display the finished products, with the artist's approval, and encourage a supportive and respectful discussion of the results.

Other Options and Extensions

Brainstorm as a group: "What variables might affect the quality of the chromatogram or the time needed to separate? Water temperature? Sort of paper used? Sort of liquid used (e.g., what if we substituted vegetable oil or milk for the water)?" Allow student groups to explore ways to vary the quality and time. Be sure that students have plenty of materials at their disposal. Have each group share its findings in classwide presentations. Ask, "What did you learn about chromatography? What did you learn about colors and the mixing of colors?"

Look into methods of coloring fabric using batik or tie dye. Using those methods, encourage students to create colorful shirts, puppets, greeting cards, or other fabric projects.

Resources

Barber, J. 1985. *Crime lab chemistry—Teachers' guide*. Berkeley, CA: Great Explorations in Math and Science (GEMS).

Beals, J. 1994. See spot run: Elementary lessons on chromatography. *Science and Children* 31 (4): 28–30.

Coleman, D., and P. B. Hounshell. 1982. Fun with paper chromatography. *Science and Children* 20 (2): 28–29.

Jenkins, C. L. 1986. Kool-aid chromatography. *Science and Children* 23 (7): 25–27.

Olshansky, B. 1990. *Portfolio of illustrated step-by-step art projects for young children*. West Nyack, NY: Center for Applied Research in Education.

Paulson, D. R. 1995. *Identification of water soluble marking pen ink*. Unpublished manuscript.

Scharmann, L. C. 1984. Autumn leaf chromatography. *Science and Children* 22 (1): 11–13.

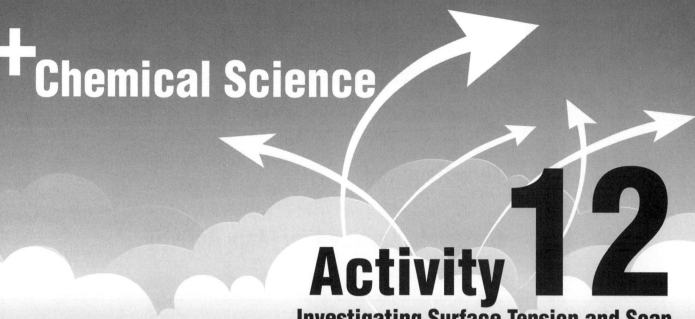

Overview

Your students encounter soap and water every day and the activity in this chapter helps them learn something new about both substances. Students find out why water can actually overfill a cup without spilling and why soap makes dust or dirt particles seem to run away. The key to both phenomena is surface tension, which is easily investigated by all grade levels using simple materials. In the process, students collect data, compute averages, graph results, and reach conclusions.

Processes/Skills

- Observing
- Predicting
- Describing
- Analyzing
- Counting
- Calculating
- Graphing
- Communicating
- Reasoning
- Applying
- Cooperating

Recommended For

Grades K–4: Small group or whole class instruction

For students in grades K–1, limit the activity to demonstration, that is, to Procedures 1, 2, and 4, making sure to engage their observation skills throughout. Assist students in constructing bar graphs of pennies used in Procedure 2.

Time Required

1–2 hours

Materials Required for Main Activity

- Water
- Clear, small plastic cups
- Pennies (or other small, standardized masses)
- Liquid soap or detergent
- Graph paper
- Colored, dustlike substance, such as graphite powder (available from hardware stores), ground pepper, or colored chalk dust
- Paper towels

Connecting to the Standards

NSES
Grades K–4 Content Standards:
Standard B: Physical Science

- Properties of objects and materials (especially noticing the observable properties of objects and materials)

Standard D: Earth and Space Science

- Properties of Earth materials (especially studying the physical and chemical properties of water)

NCTM
Standards for Grades PreK–2, 3–5:

- Numbers and Operations (especially understanding and using numbers, operations, and estimation)
- Reasoning and Proof (especially developing, selecting, and evaluating arguments and proofs)
- Communication (especially analyzing, organizing, and expressing their thinking clearly to peers and teachers)

CHEMICAL SCIENCE

Safety Considerations

Basic classroom safety practices apply.

Activity Objectives

In the following activity, students

- carry out their own investigations of surface tension and draw conclusions from their data; and

- understand how soap affects surface tension.

Background Information

The molecules within the bulk of a liquid are attracted to one another in all directions, resulting in a neutral overall force on any single molecule of that liquid. At the surface of the liquid, however, the molecules are attracted only inward and sideways, causing the surface to exhibit a tension or a skin-like quality, which is known as *surface tension*. Surface tension causes a liquid surface to act as if a membrane were stretched over it, allowing us to gently float a needle or a paper clip on water. Surface tension causes the molecules in dripping water to pull together and form drops. It also causes wet paint-brush bristles to cling together (they won't cling when dry). Soap reduces water's surface tension and reduces water's cling on small particles, such as dust or dirt, by getting in between the water molecules and the dirt molecules. This enables the dirt molecules to become suspended in the water, where they can easily be washed away.

Main Activity, Step-by-Step Procedures

1. Begin the class with a demonstration: Show students a full cup of water (best to use a clear cup or glass, filled right up to the rim). Ask, "How many pennies do you predict that I can place in the water before it overflows?" Record student predictions. Gently drop pennies into the water (edgewise works best here) until the water actually overflows the rim of the cup. You will probably use more pennies than either you or the students expect, so be sure to have plenty on hand. The water will actually rise above the rim of the cup, forming a dome-like bulge. When the water finally spills over and the demonstration is complete, give student groups a few minutes to discuss what they've seen, and ask them to explain what happened. (The water in the cup was able to rise above the rim and accommodate so many pennies due to the water's surface tension [see Background Information].)

SCIENCE
Properties of Earth
materials

MATH
Numbers and
operations

STANDARDS

MATH
Reasoning and proof

MATH
Communication

SCIENCE
Properties of objects and
materials

2. Add a single drop of liquid soap or detergent to the surface of the water in the cup, then try the same process. Ask for student predictions regarding the number of pennies it will take for the water to spill out, and then carry out the demonstration. You should find that you need far fewer pennies this time. Graph the number of pennies used in each case (bar graph), and ask students to try to explain why the soap lowered the number of pennies needed.

3. Give student groups time and materials to try the penny demonstrations (with and without soap) on their own. Students should make predictions, collect data (number of pennies), and graph their results using Activity Sheet 12.1 (p. 113). Students can then compare class results (averages) and try to answer these questions: "What effect did the soap have on the water? How do you know?"

4. As a final step, demonstrate the following for the class: Float some dust (any sort of colored dust will do) on water. Add a single drop of soap to the water. Ask students to observe what happens. (The dust particles will move quickly away from the drop of soap.) As students consider the effects caused by soap in this and the previous demonstrations, ask them if they can offer any explanations for why soap is used as a cleaning agent.

Discussion Questions

Ask students the following:

1. What allows the water to rise above the rim of the cup or glass as pennies are added?

2. What effect did the drop of soap have on the number of pennies added to the water? How do you explain this?

3. Based on what you've observed about soap, water, and dust particles, why is soap able to get us clean?

Assessment

Suggestions for specific ways to assess student understanding are provided in parentheses.

1. Did students successfully carry out their own investigations of surface tension? (Use embedded observations during Procedure 3 as performance assessment.)

2. Were students able to successfully graph, analyze, and draw conclu-

sions from their data? (Use your observations during Procedures 2 and 3 as embedded evidence, and use their responses to the Discussion Questions as prompts for science journal entries.)

3. Were students able to understand how soap affects surface tension? (Note their responses during Procedure 4 as embedded evaluation and use Discussion Question 3 as a prompt for a science journal entry.)

RUBRIC 12.1
Sample rubric using these assessment options

	Achievement Level		
	Developing 1	Proficient 2	Exemplary 3
Did students successfully carry out their own investigations of surface tension?	Attempted investigations but not successfully	Carried out investigations successfully	Carried out investigations successfully and were able to clearly discuss the experience
Were students able to successfully graph, analyze, and draw conclusions from their data?	Attempted to graph, analyze, and draw conclusions but not successfully	Successfully graphed, analyzed, and drew conclusions from their data	Successfully graphed, analyzed, and drew extensive conclusions from their data
Were students able to understand how soap affects surface tension?	Attempted to understand but were unable to offer a reasonable explanation	Were able to explain soap's effect	Were able to draw extensively from their investigatory experiences as they explained soap's effect

Other Options and Extensions

1. Ask students to conduct research on soap to determine what it is made of and how it works.

2. Encourage students to design and carry out experiments involving various soaps. Ask them, "How effective is a particular type of soap at cleaning different sorts of dirt?" Tell students to compare several different soaps in terms of how effective the soaps are in removing a particular type of dirt or stain.

3. Have students think of other ways we encounter or use surface tension (e.g., it allows a sponge to soak up water).

Resources

Barnes, G. 1978. Drops, sieves, and paintbrushes: Teaching about surface tension. *Science and Children* 15 (4): 28–29.

Blume, S. C., and P. C. Beisenherz. 1970. Turning your class on to cohesion. *Science and Children* 24 (7): 20–21.

Craig, A., and C. Rosney. 1988. *The Usborne science encyclopedia.* Tulsa, OK: EDC.

Donalson-Sams, M. 1987. Surface tension: The ways of water. *Science and Children* 25 (3): 26–28.

Kessler, J. 2003. What causes water's surface tension. *Science and Children* 40 (8): 21.

MacKinnon, G. R. 1998. Soap and science. *Science and Children* 35 (5): 28–31.

Russell, S. J., and J. Mokros. 1996. What do children understand about average? *Teaching Children Mathematics* 2 (6): 360–365.

Tolley, K. 1994. *The art and science connection.* Menlo Park, CA: Addison-Wesley.

ACTIVITY SHEET 12.1
Investigating Surface Tension and Soap

1. How many pennies will it take to make the water overflow the container?

Prediction	Actual

2. How many pennies will it take to make the water overflow the container if a drop of soap is added to the water?

Prediction	Actual

On a separate piece of paper or the back of this sheet, make a bar graph of the results above.

3. Group work: Count the number of pennies it takes to make the water overflow.

	Prediction	Actual	Your Average	Class Average
Water only	Trial 1: Trial 2: Trial 3:	Trial 1: Trial 2: Trial 3:		
Water and a single drop of soap	Trial 1: Trial 2: Trial 3:	Trial 1: Trial 2: Trial 3:		

What effect did the soap have on the water? How do you know?

4. What happened to the dust floating on the water when the drop of soap was added?

Considering the effects caused by soap in these demonstrations, can you offer any explanations about why soap is used as a cleaning agent?

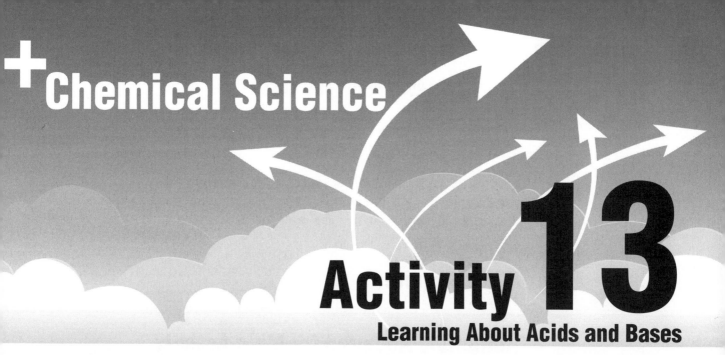

Activity 13
Learning About Acids and Bases

Overview

The chemistry of acids and bases is a fundamental area of study in the physical sciences. The following activity is really two exercises in one. First, students learn to distinguish between acids and bases using various color-changing indicator solutions. Second, students use their new knowledge of indicators to determine the relative acidity of several everyday foods. The lessons involve data collection, problem solving, and quantitative reasoning as students learn how chemists work with acids and bases.

Processes/Skills

- Ordering
- Predicting
- Measuring/counting
- Comparing
- Investigating
- Describing
- Explaining
- Cooperating
- Asking questions
- Recognizing patterns
- Communicating

Recommended For

Grades 3–4: Small group and whole class instruction
This activity can be simplified for grade 3 students by undertaking only

LEARNING ABOUT ACIDS AND BASES

the portion described in Procedures 1–4 and Activity Sheet 13.1 (p. 123). Activity Sheet 13.2 (p. 124; Procedure 5) is recommended for the more experienced students in this age range or for younger students with a good deal of adult assistance.

Time Required

2–3 hours

Materials Required for Main Activity

- Splash-proof safety goggles
- Vinegar, diluted (mixed 50:50 with water)
- Water
- Orange juice
- Baking soda
- Ammonia, diluted (mixed 10:90 with water)
- Measuring instruments (e.g., beaker, graduated cylinder, spoons, balance)
- Droppers or drinking straws
- Clear, medium-size plastic cups
- Cookie sheets or aluminum foil
- Red (purple) cabbage
- Turmeric powder
- Grape juice
- Plastic spoons
- A variety of fruits and vegetables (e.g., corn, peas, carrots, tomatoes, peaches, pineapples, apples, cherries, oranges, lemons)

Connecting to the Standards

NSES
Grades K–4 Content Standards:
Standard A: Science as Inquiry

- Abilities necessary to do scientific inquiry (especially making good

observations, using data to construct a good explanation, and communicating their ideas)

- Understanding about scientific inquiry (especially developing explanations using evidence)

Standard B: Physical Science

- Properties of objects and materials (especially noticing the observable properties of objects and materials)

NCTM
Standards for Grades PreK–2, 3–5:

- Numbers and Operations (especially understanding and using numbers and operations)

- Reasoning and Proof (especially developing, selecting, and evaluating arguments and proofs)

- Communication (especially analyzing, organizing, and expressing their thinking clearly to peers and teachers)

Safety Considerations

Basic classroom safety practices apply. Students should wear splash-proof safety goggles throughout these exercises. Exercise caution when handling all materials. Be sure that students do not ingest any chemicals found in the lab, or even touch their hands to their mouths after handling any chemicals. Students should have no direct contact (i.e., no touching) with vinegar or ammonia; the teacher should do the mixing and pouring. As an alternative, consider investigating the acids via a teacher-led demonstration.

Activity Objectives

In the following activity, students

- differentiate between acids and bases, based on color changes in indicator solutions; and

- rank order the food juices in terms of their acidity or alkalinity.

Background Information

Acids and bases are important compounds that are chemical opposites of each other in many ways and that neutralize each other when mixed. Acids are often thought of as chemicals that can harm us by burning the skin, and bases are often thought of as chemicals that are bitter and have a slip-

LEARNING ABOUT ACIDS AND BASES

pery feel. Chemists use various indicators (such as litmus paper) to determine whether substances are alkaline (i.e., basic) or acidic. When aqueous solutions of acids and bases are mixed in the proper proportions, the resulting solution (composed of water and a salt) is neutral—the solution does not demonstrate the characteristics of either an acid *or* a base.

Main Activity, Step-by-Step Procedures

1. In the next portion of the lesson, students test four commonly encountered acids and bases. Prepare the following solutions ahead of time:

    *   Vinegar (acid)—mix 50:50 with water

    *   Orange juice (acid)—no dilution necessary

    *   Baking soda (base)—about 30 g, which is about 15 ml mixed into 250 ml of water

    *   Ammonia (base)—mix 10:90 with water

    These acidic and basic solutions will be combined with various indicators, detailed in Procedure 4.

2. Prepare the following indicator solutions ahead of time:

    *   Cabbage juice: Quarter and grate a red cabbage (half a cabbage is sufficient for an entire class). Place the cabbage into a saucepan, cover with water, and boil for about five minutes. Strain out the water/juice mixture into another container and keep it in the refrigerator. This cabbage solution will be blue, but it will turn red when mixed with an acid and green when mixed with a base. If you add acid, then base, the cabbage juice will go from blue to red and back to blue.

    *   Turmeric: Mix 5 ml of turmeric powder (this spice is available in most grocery stores) into 120 ml of water. The spice won't dissolve completely, but that's okay. The turmeric solution will change from yellow to reddish brown when a base is added. However, the original solution won't change color when an acid is added. To test for the presence of an acid, you must first add a base to the turmeric solution, which turns the solution reddish-brown. The addition of an acid then will return the liquid to its original color.

    *   Grape juice: Grape juice is naturally acidic and will turn green when a base is added. To test for an acid, first add a base to turn

SCIENCE
Abilities necessary to do scientific inquiry
Properties of objects and materials

MATH
Numbers and operations

the solution green, and then add the acid to return it to its original color.

3. Begin by asking students what they know and what they want to know about acids and bases. Offer a basic definition for the terms *acid* and *base* (see Background Information). Provide students with some examples (common acids: vinegar, orange juice; common bases: baking soda, ammonia). Ask students, "Do each of the examples of acids and bases fit the general definitions?" Encourage student questions and ideas as you check for comprehension.

4. Working together in small groups, students test each of the four acids and bases using the three indicator solutions. First, students place small amounts (a few milliliters) of each of the three indicators into clear plastic cups (to observe color changes more easily) placed on top of a cookie sheet or a sheet of aluminum foil to keep desks clean. Each group needs 4 cups of each indicator (one for each of the 4 acids/bases, for a total of 12 cups), and each cup should be labeled with the name of the indicator solution it contains. Next, students add to each indicator sample a small amount (a few milliliters, using a dropper or a drinking straw with one finger held over the open end, to transfer the liquid) of each acid or base solution (vinegar, orange juice, baking soda, ammonia) and record color change findings on Activity Sheet 13.1 (p. 123). Students should get a sense of how the acids and bases react to the presence of the indicators.

When student groups complete these investigations, ask them what they learned about acids, bases, and indicators so far. Check for comprehension and clarify concepts if they are confused about some points.

5. Although most foods are somewhat acidic, they are not all equally so. In this portion of the lesson, student groups rank order several fruits and vegetables based on their levels of acidity by using the three indicator solutions. Students count the number of teaspoons of food juice needed to generate an acidic color change in an indicator (in this case, cabbage juice). The *fewer* teaspoons added, the *more acidic* the food. Remember that the rank order for acidity is also the opposite of the rank order of alkalinity, because by definition, high acidity equals low alkalinity and vice versa. Conversely, the *more* teaspoons of indicator added to the food, the *more alkaline* it is, and the *less acidic*.

SCIENCE
Understanding about scientific inquiry

MATH
Communication

MATH
Reasoning and proof

LEARNING ABOUT ACIDS AND BASES

Prepare several food juices ahead of time (using a blender and adding enough water to make each specimen "juicy"). Activity Sheet 13.2 (p. 124) is organized for five such food juices. Suggested options include corn, peas, carrots, tomatoes, peaches, pineapples, apples, cherries, and lemons. Label each juice storage container.

Ask students to predict the order of juice acidity, from most to least acidic, recording their responses on Activity Sheet 13.2A. Each student group should then place five teaspoons of cabbage juice indicator into labeled, clear plastic cups, and stir in each of the specimen food juices with a plastic spoon, one spoonful at a time, until the cabbage indicator changes color. Groups then record that number of spoonfuls for each specimen juice in Activity Sheet 13.2B. This procedure can, of course, also be conducted using the turmeric and/ or grape juice indicator solutions. Again, perform all activities on a cookie sheet or a sheet of aluminum foil, and be sure that students understand that they must not ingest any of the liquids.

Finally, each group can determine the actual order of food juice acidity on Activity Sheet 13.2C. Let each group present their results to the class by describing what they learned about acids and bases in this lesson.

Discussion Questions
Ask students the following:

1. How does an acid differ from a base? How can you tell the difference between the two?

2. Why shouldn't you touch your hands to your mouth, eyes, or nose after handling chemicals?

3. How were you able to tell which food juices were most acidic?

Assessment
Suggestions for specific ways to assess student understanding are provided in parentheses.

1. Were students able to successfully record the color changes that occurred when the vinegar, orange juice, baking soda, and ammonia were added to the four indicator solutions? (Use embedded observations made during Procedure 3 and the resulting documentation in Activity Sheet 13.1 as performance assessment.)

2. Could students differentiate between acids and bases, based on color changes in indicator solutions? (Use student responses to Discussion Question 2 as an embedded assessment or as a prompt for a science journal entry.)

3. Were students able to rank order the food juices in terms of their acidity? (Use responses to Discussion Question 3, during Procedure 5, as embedded evaluation; the results of Activity Sheet 13.2 as performance assessment; and Discussion Question 3 as a prompt for a science journal entry.)

RUBRIC 13.1
Sample rubric using these assessment options

	Achievement Level		
	Developing 1	Proficient 2	Exemplary 3
Were students able to successfully record the color changes that occurred when the vinegar, orange juice, baking soda, and ammonia were added to the three indicator solutions?	Attempted but unable to recognize and record the color changes on the Activity Sheet	Successfully recorded color changes on the Activity Sheet	Successfully recorded color changes on the Activity Sheet, and could readily explain their methods and rationales
Could students differentiate between acids and bases, based on color changes in indicator solutions?	Attempted but unable to differentiate	Successfully differentiated between acids and bases using indicator solutions	Successfully differentiated between acids and bases using indicator solutions and could readily explain their methods and rationales
Were students able to rank order the food juices in terms of their acidity?	Attempted but unable to rank order the juices	Successfully rank ordered the juices	Successfully rank ordered the juices and could readily explain their methods and rationales

Other Options and Extensions

1. Ask students to test baking powder with an indicator solution for acidity or alkalinity (e.g., cabbage juice). Baking powder is actually a combination of sodium bicarbonate and a powdered acid; when moistened the two combine and release carbon dioxide gas to make the food rise. Ask students, "What happens when the liquid is added to the dry baking powder?"

2. Have students test various soaps and cleansers using cabbage juice and then rank order the results.

3. Ask students to bring in examples of their favorite foods to test for acid/base.

Resources

Damante, K. 2004. Understanding acid rain. *Science and Children* 12 (3): 53–54.

Linens, G. E. 2004. What is acid rain? *Science and Children* 12 (3): 52.

Longfield, J. 2006. Safety first: Building safety lessons into a third-grade acid-base exploration. *Science and Children* 43 (5): 26–27.

McBride, J. W. 1995. Acid tests and basic fun. *Science and Children* 33 (4): 26–27.

Robertson, B. 2006. Why does a color change indicate a chemical change? *Science and Children* 43 (5): 48–49.

Tolley, K. 1994. *The art and science connection.* Menlo Park, CA: Addison-Wesley.

Townsend, J., and K. Burton. 2006. Indicators for inquiry. *Science and Children* 43 (5): 37–41.

CHEMICAL SCIENCE

ACTIVITY SHEET 13.1
Learning About Acids and Bases

1. In each box, record any color changes that occurred when the acid or base was added to the indicator solutions.

Indicators

Acids and Bases	Cabbage Juice	Turmeric	Grape Juice
Vinegar (acid)			
Orange Juice (acid)			
Baking Soda (base)			
Ammonia (base)			

2. Conclusions: What did you learn about acid-base indicators? Which was most effective? How do you know?

LEARNING ABOUT ACIDS AND BASES

ACTIVITY SHEET 13.2
Learning About Acids and Bases

Indicator Solution used: _____.

A. Rank order the juices in terms of their acidity. First, make your predictions, then carry out the experiments and list the actual order based on your data.

	Predicted
Most Acidic (Least Alkaline):	1.
	2.
	3.
	4.
Least Acidic (Most Alkaline):	5.

B. Record the number of spoonfuls used to cause a color change in the indicator solution.

Juices Tested	Number of Spoonfuls Used

C. What was the actual rank order of acidity, based on your data in part B?

	Actual
Most Acidic (Least Alkaline):	1.
	2.
	3.
	4.
Least Acidic (Most Alkaline):	5.

Conclusions:

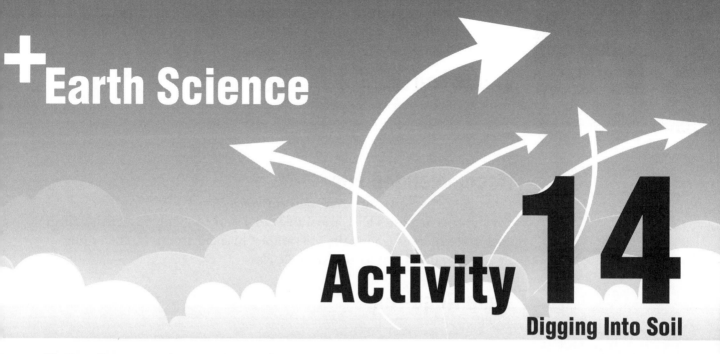

Earth Science

Activity 14
Digging Into Soil

Overview

For this Earth science investigation, students examine the composition of soil samples taken from three different depths at the same location. Students answer questions such as "How do the three samples compare? How does the soil feel? Look? Smell? What sorts of things are included in it? Are there any living creatures? Will a hand lens help me find out?" Students measure, count, and graph the number of rocks greater than or equal to 3 cm in diameter. Finally, they estimate the percentages of seven soil components for each of the three samples.

Processes/Skills

- Observing
- Predicting
- Measuring
- Counting
- Describing
- Graphing
- Analyzing
- Comparing
- Concluding
- Cooperating
- Communicating

Recommended For

Grades K–4: Small group and whole class instruction
For students in grades K–1, use Tables 14.1 and 14.2 only in Activity Sheet 14.1 (p. 132), investigating the soil samples in small groups but recording the data on the chalkboard as a whole class.

Time Required

1–2 hours

Materials Required for Main Activity

- Soil samples (from three depths: 3 cm, 50 cm, and 1 m)
- Beaker or other measuring device (you can make serviceable "beakers" by measuring out 250 ml of water in a real beaker or measuring cup, pouring it into a clear plastic cup, and marking the 250 ml level on that container)
- Hand lenses (5× or 10× are adequate)
- Markers or pens
- Large plastic cups
- Metric rulers
- Graph paper
- Newsprint or butcher paper

Connecting to the Standards

NSES
Grades K–4 Content Standards:
Standard A: Science as Inquiry

- Abilities necessary to do scientific inquiry (especially making good observations, using data to construct a good explanation, and communicating their ideas)

Standard D: Earth and Space Science

- Properties of Earth materials (especially studying the physical properties of rocks, soil, and some of the organisms that live in soil)

NCTM
Standards for Grades PreK–2, 3–5:

- Numbers and Operations (especially understanding and using numbers, operations, and estimation)

- Reasoning and Proof (especially developing, selecting, and evaluating arguments and proofs)

- Communication (especially analyzing, organizing, and expressing their thinking clearly to peers and teachers)

- Representation (especially using graphic representations to model phenomena and solve problems)

Safety Considerations
Basic classroom safety practices apply.

Activity Objectives
In the following activity, students

- describe, compare, and reach conclusions about the composition of the three soil samples; and

- estimate component percentages of the three soil samples.

Background Information
The texture of a soil is determined by the size of its constituent particles, which are classified, based on size, as gravel, sand, silt, or clay. Gravel particles are larger than 2.0 mm in diameter. Sand particles are easily seen, feel gritty, and range in size from 0.05 nm to 2.0 mm. Silt particles feel like flour, can barely be seen by the unaided eye, and range in size from 0.002 nm to 0.05 mm. Clay particles are too fine to be seen with the unaided eye and are difficult to see even under a microscope.

Collect the soil samples at school if possible; students can help dig and measure depth. If this is not feasible, collect the soil yourself and bring in sufficient samples from the three depths. Be sure to replace the soil at, or at least near, the appropriate depth (for the sake of the organisms involved) when done with the activity.

Main Activity, Step-by-Step Procedures
1. Ask students what they know about soil: "Is it the same thing as dirt? Does soil matter to us? Why or why not? Have you ever taken a close

MATH
Numbers and operations
Representation
Reasoning and proof
Communication

look at soil?" Explain to students that they will look closely at soil from the same location but from three different depths: 3 cm, 50 cm, and 1 m. Ask students, "What do you think you'll observe? Will the soil samples vary at the three depths? How will they vary?" Have students record their predictions in Table 14.1 on Activity Sheet 14.1. Ask students what they expect to find in terms of texture, color, odor, inclusions (e.g., rocks and sticks), life-forms, and other factors.

Give each group a hand lens and a 250 ml sample (use a beaker to measure, loosely packed) of the surface soil (top 3 cm) in a large plastic cup or other suitable container and have them make and record their observations in Table 14.1 on the Activity Sheet. Repeat with the 50 cm depth and the 1 m depth soil samples. Be sure that groups keep all three samples (mark the cups accordingly). After students observe all three samples, ask students to describe what they found. Ask, "Did you see what you expected to see? How did your predictions differ from your actual observations?"

2. In this procedure, students count and compare the number of rock inclusions in each of the three samples. Direct student groups to count the number of rocks greater than or equal to 3 cm in diameter (they will need a metric ruler) in each sample and record the data in Table 14.2. Have each group make a bar graph of the number of rocks counted in each of the three samples. Ask students, "What conclusions can you reach by looking at your data represented in graphic form? Do you find that the bar graph helps make sense of the data? How?" Students may respond that it is easier to understand the evidence when they can see it represented in a bar graph.

Ask students to describe the components of the soil samples. Encourage qualitative and quantitative responses. Offer descriptions of *gravel, silt, sand,* and *clay* (see Background Information). Direct each group to spread out each sample, one sample at a time, on a large sheet of plain paper (newsprint or butcher paper). For each sample, have students estimate the percentage of each sample that is rock, gravel, sand, silt, clay, organic material, and other substances. Students may find it useful to try separating those component parts, at least roughly, to help with the estimation process. Students should record their estimates in Table 14.3. Ask them, "What can you conclude from your data? What else would you like to know about soil?"

Discussion Questions

Ask students the following:

1. How were your observations of the soil different from what you expected to find?

2. Which soil depth contained the most rocks? How do you know?

3. How can you tell the difference between the different soil components?

Assessment

Suggestions for specific ways to assess student understanding are provided in parentheses.

1. Were students able to effectively describe what they observed in the soil samples and compare their predictions to what they actually observed? (Use student responses to Discussion Questions 1 and 2 during the activity as embedded evidence, or use those questions as prompts for science journal entries.)

2. Could students reach meaningful conclusions about the differences between the three different samples? (Use Discussion Question 3 during the activity or concluding analysis as an embedded assessment or as a science journal entry.)

3. Were students able to successfully estimate component percentages of the samples? (Observe student activity during Procedure 3 and use that embedded evidence as a form of performance assessment.)

RUBRIC 14.1
Sample rubric using these assessment options

	Achievement Level		
	Developing 1	Proficient 2	Exemplary 3
Were students able to effectively describe what they observed in the soil samples and compare their predictions to what they actually observed?	Attempted but were unable to adequately make this comparison	Successfully described their soil samples and compared those observations with predicted outcomes	Successfully and extensively described their soil samples and comprehensively compared those observations with predicted outcomes
Could students reach meaningful conclusions about the differences between the three different samples?	Attempted but were unsuccessful in reaching meaningful conclusions	Successfully communicated meaningful conclusions regarding the three soil samples	Successfully communicated meaningful conclusions regarding the three soil samples, including significant discussion of quantitative data
Were students able to successfully estimate component percentages of the samples?	Attempted this estimation but unsuccessfully	Successfully estimated the component percentages	Successfully estimated the component percentages, including significant discussion of quantitative data

Other Options and Extensions

1. Students can collect and compare soil samples from different locations: various spots around the school grounds, the neighborhood, students' yards, and nearby natural areas. Students can also conduct research, via the library or internet, on how soil varies around the world.

2. Ask students to use the internet or library to investigate the importance of soil in agriculture.

3. Students can also conduct research on what types of organisms live in the soil.

Resources

Barcus, S., and M. M. Patton. 1996. What's the matter? *Science and Children* 34 (1): 49.

Danisa, D., J. Gentile, K. McNamara, M. Pinney, S. Ross, and A. Rule. 2006. Geoscience for preschoolers. *Science and Children* 44 (4): 30–33.

Gibb, L. 2000. Second-grade soil scientists. *Science and Children* 38 (3): 24–28.

Varelas, M., and J. Benhart. 2004. Welcome to rock day. *Science and Children* 41 (4): 40–45.

Whiten, D. J., and P. Whiten. 2003. Talk counts: Discussing graphs with young children. *Teaching Children Mathematics* 10 (3): 142–149.

Yang, D. 2006. Developing number sense through real-life situations. *Teaching Children Mathematics* 13 (2): 104–106.

DIGGING INTO SOIL

ACTIVITY SHEET 14.1
Digging Into Soil

TABLE 14.1
Soil observations

Soil Sample	Predictions: What do you think you'll observe?	Actual Observations					
		Texture	Color	Odor	Inclusions	Life-Forms	Other
Top 3 cm							
50 cm deep							
1 m deep							

How did your predictions differ from your actual observations?

TABLE 14.2
How many rocks (≥ 3 cm in diameter) were in each sample?

Soil Sample	Number of Rocks
Top 3 cm	
50 cm deep	
1 m deep	

On a separate piece of paper or on the back of this sheet, make a bar graph of your data.

TABLE 14.3
Estimate the component percentages of each sample.

Soil Sample	Estimated Percentages						
	Rock	Gravel	Sand	Silt	Clay	Organic	Other
Top 3 cm							
50 cm deep							
1 m deep							

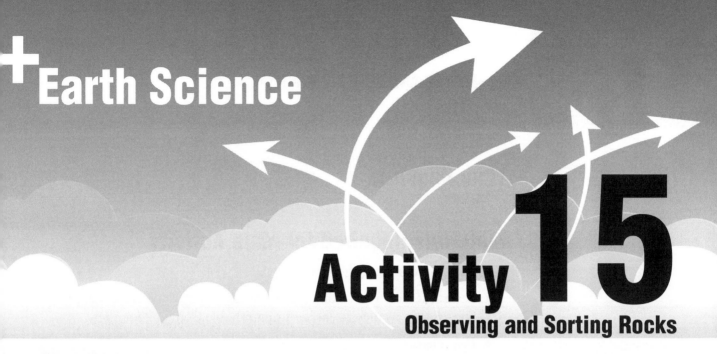

Activity 15
Observing and Sorting Rocks

Overview

In this activity, students examine garden variety rocks, classifying them based on observable properties. This lesson teaches students not only about rocks but also about how to take a closer look at objects and materials that they encounter every day. Students are encouraged to notice details that they may have previously overlooked. Students observe, test, and sort a collection of rocks using a variety of criteria including hardness, texture, luster, reaction to weak acid, magnetic attraction, and density. They then use Venn diagrams to group similar rocks.

Processes/Skills

- Observing
- Describing
- Measuring
- Classifying
- Analyzing
- Recognizing patterns
- Problem solving
- Comparing
- Cooperating

Recommended For

Grades K–4: Small group or whole class instruction
This activity can be adapted for grades K–2 by conducting Procedures 1 and 2 as a hands-on investigation. You can also make the simpler aspects of Procedures 3–5 a teacher-led, whole class exercise (adjust to your students' skill levels).

Time Required

2–3 hours

Materials Required for Main Activity

- Splash-proof safety goggles
- Several sets of 5 to 10 different rocks (garden variety specimens are fine, as long as they're easily distinguishable from one another)
- Hand lenses
- Masking tape
- Metric rulers
- Vinegar
- Droppers or drinking straws
- Magnets
- Metric balances
- Beaker or graduated cylinder

Materials Required for Going Further

- Rocks
- A variety of construction materials such as tape, cardboard, paper, scissors, sticks, glue, and string

Connecting to the Standards

NSES
Grades K–4 Content Standards:
Standard A: Science as Inquiry

- Abilities necessary to do scientific inquiry (especially making good observations, using data to construct a good explanation, and communicating their ideas)
- Understanding about scientific inquiry (especially developing explanations using good evidence)

Standard D: Earth and Space Science

- Properties of Earth materials (especially studying the physical properties of rocks)

NCTM
Standards for Grades PreK–2, 3–5:

- Numbers and Operations (especially understanding and using numbers and operations)

- Reasoning and Proof (especially developing, selecting, and evaluating arguments and proofs)

- Communication (especially analyzing, organizing, and expressing their thinking clearly to peers and teachers)

- Representation (especially using graphic representations to model phenomena and solve problems)

Safety Considerations

Basic classroom safety practices apply. Splash-proof safety goggles are required when working with vinegar, or minimize the risks by presenting the vinegar test as a teacher demonstration only.

Activity Objectives

In the following activity, students

- sort rocks into several categories based on their own criteria;

- test rocks for various properties, including hardness, reaction to acid, magnetic attraction, luster, texture, and density; and

- use Venn diagrams to group rocks.

Background Information

About Rocks

Rocks are *aggregates* (combinations or composites) of *minerals* (naturally occurring inorganic, or nonliving, substances, each with a definite chemical composition). Rocks are often classified into three main groups:

1. *Igneous rocks* are formed from molten magma and make up most of the continental crust; examples include pumice and granite.

OBSERVING AND SORTING ROCKS

2. *Sedimentary rocks* are formed on Earth's surface, usually as products of erosion from other rocks; that is, rocks erode, and the debris becomes deposited into low-lying areas where in time it is compacted into new sorts of rocks. Examples include sandstone, shale, and limestone.

3. *Metamorphic rocks* are formed by alteration of other rocks by heat, pressure, and other natural forces; an example is mica.

About Venn Diagrams

A Venn diagram is a graphic form of representation, using intersecting circles to indicate relationships between sets, in this case, groups of rocks. Venn diagrams are particularly useful in identifying similarities and differences within and between groups of objects. In this activity they help students organize their geological observations in order to reach conclusions about rock samples.

Main Activity, Step-by-Step Procedures

SCIENCE

Abilities necessary to do
  scientific inquiry
Properties of Earth
  materials

MATH

Numbers and operations

1. Ask, "Are rocks important to people? How do we use rocks?" As students respond, be sure they realize that humans have long used rocks for many purposes including tools, ornaments, and building materials. Ask students if they can think of any other uses for rocks, where they have seen rocks, and to describe some rocks they've seen. Have students answer the following questions: "How do the rocks differ from one another? What do rocks have in common? Size? Color? Other characteristics? Where do you think rocks come from? Why are rocks important to us?"

2. Give each student group a collection of 5 to 10 different rocks, a metric ruler, and a hand lens. Each rock should have its own number (marked on a small piece of masking tape). Each group's collection can contain different types of rocks, as long as there is a variety in each set. Give students a few minutes to just observe their rocks, and then ask them to sort the rocks into two piles based on some characteristic they notice about the rocks. One student from each group should document the sorting criteria. Discuss their ideas: Did they sort the rocks based on size (large or small), color (black or white), shape (flat or round), or another observable property (striped or not)? There are no wrong answers here, so you can encourage diverse and creative responses. Have each group complete this sorting process several more times and keep a written record of their sorting criteria each time. Ask groups to share and discuss their sorting schemes.

3. Next, groups can test the rocks in several ways. The following tests serve as ways to classify rocks. Groups should keep a written record of their test results using Activity Sheet 15.1 (p. 141).

Hardness: Students should test the rock specimens for hardness by selecting any two rocks and scratching one against the other. The rock that leaves a scratch on the other rock is harder. Have students take the harder of the two rocks and test it against another specimen from the collection, and so on, until they determine the hardest rock. Students should find the second hardest rock, the third, and so on, until they know the order of hardness for all the rocks.

Reaction to acid: Students with rocks containing calcium carbonate—such as limestone, marble, calcite, or chalk—can do the following test. While wearing safety goggles, students place a few drops of vinegar (a weak acid) on each rock. Rocks containing calcium carbonate will fizz in the presence of vinegar, indicating a positive test.

Magnetic attraction: Does a magnet react to any of the rocks? An iron-containing rock, such as galena, will, as will a lodestone. A lodestone is made of magnetite and is a naturally occurring magnetic rock.

Luster: Luster refers to the rock's shininess, that is, its ability to reflect light. Have students check each rock to judge whether it is shiny or dull.

Texture: Have students look at the crystals or particles in the rocks, using metric rulers to measure the particles' widths. If the particles are ≥ 3 mm in size, the rock is "rough." If they are < 3 mm in size, the rock is "smooth."

Density: This test is offered as an adaptation for older or more advanced students. The density of an object refers to its relative weight and is calculated by dividing the object's mass by its volume. For each rock in the collection, ask students to find the mass in grams using a balance and divide that number by the specimen's volume in milliliters. To determine the volume, completely immerse the rock in a beaker or graduated cylinder of water and measure how many milliliters it displaces. In other words, how much higher did the water go when the rock was placed into the container? If the water was at a level of 100 ml and rose to 200 ml when the rock was immersed, then the rock has a volume of 100 ml. Tell students to rank order (first, second, third, and so on) the rock specimens based on their densities.

SCIENCE
Understanding about
  scientific inquiry

MATH
Communication
Representation

4. Instruct students to use the information gathered in Procedure 3 to decide where the rocks fit into the Venn diagram on Activity Sheet 15.1 (p. 142). Students should write each rock's number in the proper circle or junction of circles, based on whether it has a rough or smooth texture, is shiny or dull in luster, and/or reacts to vinegar. Some rocks (those that are smooth, dull, and do not react to vinegar) might not fit into any circles; they should be placed outside all three Venn circles. When students have finished, discuss their completed Venn diagrams. Ask, "Which rocks in the collection were most similar? How do you know? Why is the Venn diagram helpful in determining similarities and differences?"

Finally, student groups can make their own Venn diagrams using any bimodal (either-or) characteristics that they noticed and recorded in Procedure 2. For instance, the diagrams can include characteristics such as large or small, light or dark, striped or not, and single color or multiple colors. For younger students, a Venn diagram with two intersecting circles is appropriate (make copies ahead of time). More advanced students can try three or even four circles at once. (See Activity Sheet 15.1.)

Discuss student results as a class. Ask students, "What have you learned about rocks? What else would you like to know?" Ask each student group to write their own definition of the word *rock*. This would be a good time to introduce the concepts of igneous, sedimentary, and metamorphic rocks. Have students categorize the rocks in their collections into each of these three categories.

Discussion Questions

Ask students the following:

1. What types of characteristics do rocks have in common?

2. Which rock from the collection is your favorite? Why?

3. What other objects could you sort using a Venn diagram?

Assessment

Suggestions for specific ways to assess student understanding are provided in parentheses.

1. Were students able to sort the rocks into several categories based on their own criteria? (Use observational, embedded evidence from

Procedure 2 as performance assessment. Also use Discussion Questions 1 and 2 as prompts for science journal entries.)

2. Did students successfully test the rocks for hardness, reaction to acid, magnetic attraction, luster, texture, and density? (Use observational, embedded evidence and the results of the completed Activity Sheets as performance assessment.)

3. Were students able to comprehend and use the Venn diagrams? (Use observational, embedded evidence in Procedure 5 as performance assessment. Also use Discussion Question 3 as a prompt for a science journal entry.)

RUBRIC 15.1
Sample rubric using these assessment options

	Achievement Level		
	Developing **1**	**Proficient** **2**	**Exemplary** **3**
Were students able to sort the rocks into several categories based on their own criteria?	Attempted, but were unable to successfully sort	Successfully sorted the rocks into several categories	Successfully sorted the rocks into several categories and clearly explained their rationales for doing so
Did students successfully test the rocks for hardness, reaction to acid, magnetic attraction, luster, texture, and density?	Attempted, but were unable to successfully test the rock samples	Successfully tested the samples and recorded their findings	Successfully tested the samples, recorded their findings, and clearly explained their rationales for doing so
Were students able to comprehend and use the Venn diagrams?	Attempted, but were unable to successfully use the Venn diagrams to sort rocks	Successfully sorted rocks using the Venn diagrams	Successfully sorted rocks using the Venn diagrams and clearly explained their rationales for doing so

Going Further

For a social studies connection, have each student group choose one of their rocks and make it into a tool that a person in ancient times might have used. Offer a variety of materials for tool construction (e.g., tape, cardboard, paper, scissors, sticks, glue, string). When completed, each group can explain to the class how their tool was constructed and how it would be used. Students should look into the history of rock tools using the library or internet.

Other Options and Extensions

1. Students can begin their own rock collections, keeping track of where and when they found each specimen. Display their collections in the classroom.

2. Using reference materials, students can identify the types of rocks found in the classroom rock collections.

3. Students can search for rocks that look like other things: people's faces, cars, boats, houses, etc.

4. Ask students to investigate Mohs' scale, developed in 1812 by German mineralogist Friedrich Mohs, to determine the hardness of minerals and rocks. In increasing order of hardness: (1) talc, (2) gypsum, (3) calcite, (4) fluorite, (5) apatite, (6) orthoclase feldspar, (7) quartz, (8) topaz, (9) corundum, (10) diamond.

Resources

Barcus, S., and M. M. Patton. 1996. What's the matter? *Science and Children* 34 (1): 49.

Gaylen, N. 1998. Encouraging curiosity at home. *Science and Children* 35 (4): 24–25.

Girod, M. 2000. Rocks as windows into the past. *Science and Children* 37 (6): 40–43.

MacFall, R. P. 1980. *Rock hunter's guide.* New York: Crowell.

Pearlman, S., and K. Pericak-Spector. 1994. A series of seriation activities. *Science and Children* 31 (4): 37–39.

Sorel, K. 2003. Rock solid. *Science and Children* 40 (5): 24–29.

Varelas, M., and J. Benhart. 2004. Welcome to rock day. *Science and Children* 41(4): 40–45.

Whiten, D. J., and P. Whiten. 2003. Talk counts: Discussing graphs with young children. *Teaching Children Mathematics* 10 (3): 142–149.

ACTIVITY SHEET 15.1
Observing and Sorting Rocks

List the rocks (by their number) in order from softest to hardest:

    1.   2.   3.   4.   5.   6.   7.   8.   9.   10.

Which rock(s) reacted to the vinegar?

To which rock(s) did a magnet react?

Luster:

Shiny Rocks	Dull Rocks

Texture: Rough = crystals or particles ≥ 3 mm
                  Smooth = crystals or particles < 3 mm

Rough Rocks	Smooth Rocks

Density:

Rock #	Mass (g)	Volume (ml)	Density (mass/volume)	Rank Order

Venn Diagram

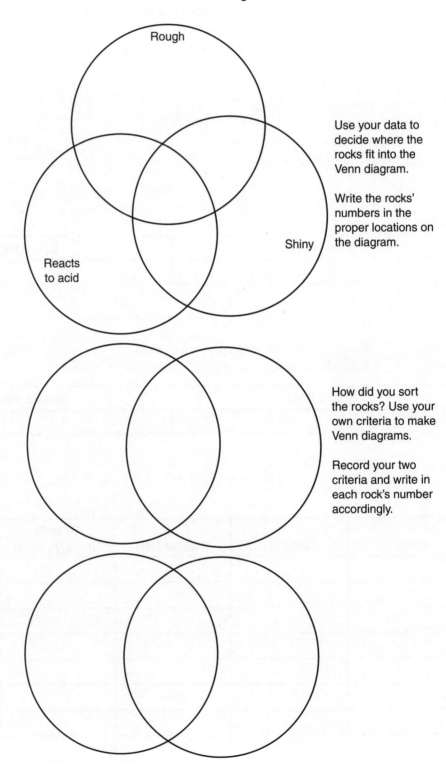

Use your data to decide where the rocks fit into the Venn diagram.

Write the rocks' numbers in the proper locations on the diagram.

How did you sort the rocks? Use your own criteria to make Venn diagrams.

Record your two criteria and write in each rock's number accordingly.

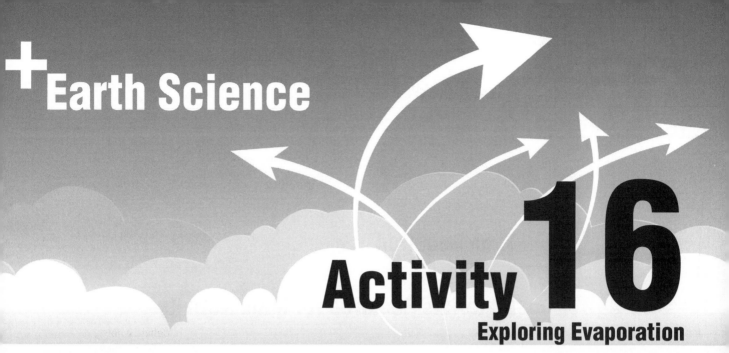

Earth Science

Activity 16
Exploring Evaporation

Overview

Students learn what evaporation is and how various factors—time, heat, surface area, and wind—affect it. They also discover that water does not always evaporate at the same rate and that saltwater leaves something behind when it evaporates. Finally, students apply what they have learned to discover how evaporation affects climate and weather.

In this activity, the "factual information" regarding evaporation is purposely distributed throughout the lesson, with much of it left for the lesson's end. By investigating first and being informed later, students remain engaged throughout the activity. The lesson begins with concrete, hands-on experiences and later merges those experiences with factual material.

Processes/Skills

- Observing
- Inquiring
- Describing
- Measuring
- Graphing
- Analyzing data
- Problem solving
- Communicating

Recommended For

Grades K–4: Small group and whole class instruction
This activity can be adapted for grades K–1 by turning Procedures 1–5 into teacher-led, whole class investigations. Procedure 6 may be included

in the teacher-led, whole class investigations as well, but you will need to simplify the vocabulary component.

Time Required

2–3 hours

Materials Required for Main Activity

- Water
- Beaker and/or graduated cylinder (for measuring)
- Small plastic cups (medicine cups work very well)
- Plastic plates
- Graph paper
- Markers or pens
- Paper towels
- Desk lamp(s)
- Aluminum foil and/or cookie sheets
- Small fan(s)
- Salt

Connecting to the Standards

NSES
Grades K–4 Content Standards:
Standard A: Science as Inquiry

- Abilities necessary to do scientific inquiry (especially making good observations, using data to construct a good explanation, and communicating their ideas)
- Understanding about scientific inquiry (especially developing explanations using good evidence)

Standard D: Earth and Space Science

- Properties of Earth materials (especially studying the physical and chemical properties of water)

NCTM
Standards for Grades PreK–2, 3–5:

- Measurement (especially understanding units and processes of measurement and measurable aspects of objects)

- Problem Solving (especially constructing new math knowledge through problem solving)

- Reasoning and Proof (especially developing, selecting, and evaluating arguments and proofs)

- Representation (especially using graphics to model phenomena and solve problems)

Safety Considerations

Basic classroom safety practices apply. The fans used in Procedure 4 must have safely enclosed blades if students carry out the experiment. If there is any doubt about the safety of the fan, you should set up the fan yourself, undertaking Procedure 4 as a demonstration for the whole class.

Activity Objectives

In the following activity, students

- define *evaporation* in their own words and explain how it may affect climate and weather;

- graph, analyze, and draw conclusions from their data regarding variables that affect evaporation; and

- explain evaporation's place in the water cycle.

Main Activity, Step-by-Step Procedures

1. Ask students whether they have ever left water out for a period of time: "What happened to the water? If it disappeared, where did it go? Do other liquids disappear this way? Do all water sources disappear like this? How about puddles, lakes, streams, seas, and oceans?" Explain that this disappearance of liquids is called *evaporation*. Evaporation is the process of a liquid changing into a gas. Ask students, "What do you want to know about evaporation? How can we find out more about evaporation?" Explain that in the upcoming series of exercises they will explore aspects of evaporation.

SCIENCE
Abilities necessary to do
  scientific inquiry
Properties of Earth
  materials

MATH
Measurement
Problem solving
Representation

EXPLORING EVAPORATION

This first part of the lesson takes a few days, so plan ahead. Begin with the question, "How fast does water evaporate?" Provide student groups with graduated cylinders or beakers, water, markers, and a small plastic cup. Have each group mark its cup at the 10, 20, 30, and 40 ml points and fill it with water up to the 40 ml mark. Place all of the groups' cups in an open, but protected, spot in the room. Students should predict how long it will take for one-fourth (10 ml), one-half (20 ml), three-fourths (30 ml), and all (40 ml) of the water in their cups to evaporate. Data can be collected daily and recorded on Activity Sheet 16.1 (p. 151). More advanced students may graph the results (volume of water on the y axis and time on the x axis). Ask students, "What conclusions did you reach? How would you define *evaporation* in your own words? Does evaporation seem fast or slow?"

2. Ask students, "Does heat affect evaporation?" Direct student groups to place 5 ml of water in each of two plates. Place one plate on a desk or countertop under a warm lamp or in direct sunlight, and the other on a desk or countertop away from the lamp and direct sunlight. Have students predict which sample will evaporate first. Students can record the actual time for each plate of water to evaporate and display the data in a bar graph.

   Hydrogen bonds between the molecules in water tend to hold the water together and keep it from evaporating quickly. Heat breaks the bonds between the liquid molecules, allowing them to break free and evaporate into the air. The more heat, the more evaporation. Ask students to think of several examples of evaporation in real life. Ask, "What is the source of heat that causes evaporation in the case of each example?"

3. Now ask, "What else might affect evaporation?" Have student groups place 5 ml of water in small plastic cups and another 5 ml of water on a cookie sheet or sheet of aluminum foil. Ask, "Which will evaporate fastest?" Students can record the time needed for each source of water to evaporate and display the data in a bar graph. Ask students to analyze their results and think about what the results show.

   Surface area is connected to evaporation rate. If the surface area is great, more water molecules are exposed to heat and more water molecules can escape from the liquid. Therefore, the greater the surface area, the greater the rate of evaporation. Anyone with long hair will tell you that it takes much longer to dry if it is tied up in a braid as opposed to being spread out over the shoulders.

4. Ask students, "Could any other factor significantly affect evaporation?" Have student groups place 5 ml of water into each of two plates and place one plate in front of a small fan and the other somewhere else (not in front of a fan). Ask, "Which will evaporate fastest?" Again, students can record the time needed for each source of water to evaporate and display the data in a bar graph. Ask, "What do these results indicate?"

Moving air (wind) clearly affects evaporation. The wind blows away the escaping water molecules, allowing more water molecules to warm and escape. More wind means more evaporation. To return to the hair drying example, remember that wet hair dries faster in a moving car with the windows down than it does indoors.

5. Most of the world's water is salty, so students might wonder, *What happens when saltwater evaporates?* Mix a tablespoon of salt into 50 ml of water and have student groups place 5 ml of the mixture onto small sheets of aluminum foil. Allow the water to evaporate completely (you could challenge students to try to speed up the evaporation rate as much as possible using what they have learned about heat, surface area, or moving air). The white residue left behind is the salt, because it cannot evaporate into the air with the water. When salty ocean or seawater evaporates, therefore, the salt stays behind.

6. Ask the class what they learned about evaporation in these exercises. List their responses on the board. Ask, "Why is evaporation important?" Encourage student responses. Explain that the chemical process we call *evaporation* is important to living things. You can feel its cooling effect, for instance, by wetting your arm and blowing air over it. Evaporation is also an important part of the water cycle (see Figure 16.1, p. 148), which keeps all of Earth's plants and animals alive. The water cycle also is the basis for climate and weather. Ask students, "Which has a greater rate of evaporation, a deep lake or a shallow lake? A cool sea or a warm sea? A hot desert or a cool prairie? How might evaporation affect an area's humidity and temperature? Why do we find monsoons and hurricanes mainly in tropical regions?" Many questions come to mind regarding evaporation. Find out what your students would like to know, and encourage them to investigate further.

SCIENCE
Understanding about
scientific inquiry

MATH
Reasoning and proof

EXPLORING EVAPORATION

FIGURE 16.1. The water cycle

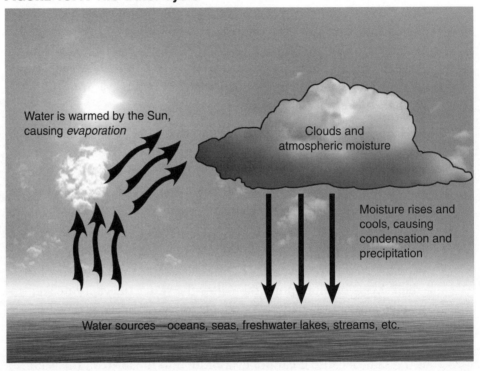

Water is warmed by the Sun, causing *evaporation*

Clouds and atmospheric moisture

Moisture rises and cools, causing condensation and precipitation

Water sources—oceans, seas, freshwater lakes, streams, etc.

Discussion Questions

Ask students the following:

1. How can we slow down the rate of evaporation? How can we speed it up?

2. How might oceans affect an area's climate and weather?

3. Why don't the oceans eventually evaporate completely?

Assessment

Suggestions for specific ways to assess student understanding are provided in parentheses.

1. Could students provide a definition for *evaporation* in their own words, as well as discuss its general effect on climate and weather? (Use observational, embedded evidence from all procedures as performance assessment. Also, use Discussion Question 2 as a prompt for a science journal entry.)

2. Were students able to successfully graph, analyze, and draw conclusions from their data regarding variables that affect evaporation? (Use observational, embedded evidence from Procedures 2–4 as performance assessment. Also use Discussion Question 1 as a prompt for a science journal entry.)

3. Do students understand evaporation's place in the water cycle? (Use feedback during Procedure 6 as embedded evidence, or use Discussion Question 3 as a prompt for a science journal entry.)

RUBRIC 16.1
Sample rubric using these assessment options

	Achievement Level		
	Developing 1	Proficient 2	Exemplary 3
Could students provide a definition for evaporation in their own words, as well as discuss its general effect on climate and weather?	Attempted but were unable to successfully define or discuss	Successfully defined evaporation and discussed its effect on climate and weather	Successfully defined evaporation and used that definition to extensively discuss its effect on climate and weather
Were students able to successfully graph, analyze, and draw conclusions from their data regarding variables that affect evaporation?	Attempted to utilize their data but were unsuccessful	Successfully graphed, analyzed, and drew basic conclusions from their data regarding variables affecting evaporation	Successfully graphed, analyzed, and drew extensive conclusions as they discussed evaporation rate and its effect on climate and weather
Do students understand evaporation's place in the water cycle?	Attempted to explain but were unsuccessful	Successfully explained evaporation's place in the water cycle	Successfully discussed evaporation's place in the water cycle, and demonstrated a thorough, working knowledge of the entire water cycle

Other Options and Extensions

1. Encourage students to explore the role of condensation in the water cycle. For example, place ice water in a metal cup and have students observe the water condensing on the cup's outer surface. Can students explain its source? Refer to the water cycle diagram (Figure 16.1).

2. Challenge students to learn more about evaporation's effect on weather and climate in their region.

Resources

Chick, L., A. S. Holmes, N. McClymonds, S. Musick, S., P. Reynolds, and G. Shultz. 2008. Weather or not. *Teaching Children Mathematics* 14 (8): 464–465.

Damonte, K. 2003. Water for life. *Science and Children* 40 (6): 45–46.

Gentile, L. 1991. The disappearing act. *Science and Children* 28 (8): 26–27.

Koziel, K. 1994. The water cycler. *Science and Children* 32 (1): 42–43.

Varelas, M., C. Pappas, A. Barry, and A. O'Neill. 2001. Examining language to capture scientific understandings: The case of the water cycle. *Science and Children* 38 (7): 26–29.

Vowell, J., and M. Phillips. 2007. A drop through time. *Science and Children* 44 (9): 30–34.

ACTIVITY SHEET 16.1
Exploring Evaporation

In the table, *predict* how long it will take for each amount of water to evaporate from the cup. Keep track of how long it *actually* takes, and then find the *difference* between the predicted and actual time by subtracting the smaller from the larger.

Volume of Water	Fraction of Volume	Time Until Evaporated		
		Predicted Time	Actual Time	Difference
10 ml	1/4			
20 ml	1/2			
30 ml	3/4			
40 ml	1/1			

Graph your results: volume of water on the *x* axis versus time on the *y* axis.

What conclusions can you draw from your data?

+Life Science

Activity 17
Examining Colors, Color Perception, and Sight

Overview

Students of all ages are fascinated by color and how we perceive it. For the main activity in this chapter, your class explores colors and visual perception by mixing colors in several ways. Students learn more about colors, light, vision, and color composition as they mix paints, spin two or more colors into new colors, and make discoveries about color perception in the human eye and brain. The preliminary activity dynamically introduces several important terms related to vision: *refraction, reflection,* and *spectrum.* Students also learn about the anatomy of the vertebrate eye, as they build and operate a simple eye model, complete with lens. In the Going Further section, the class has the opportunity to discover variables that can affect an individual's perception of color.

Processes/Skills

- Observing
- Measuring
- Predicting
- Describing
- Inferring
- Experimenting
- Communicating
- Reflecting
- Recognizing patterns
- Problem solving
- Inquiring
- Creating
- Cooperating

Recommended For

Grades K–4: Small group instruction
Adapt the lessons for grades K–2 by simplifying the vocabulary involved,
focusing your efforts on the color mixing activity (Procedure 2), and offering
the other Procedures as teacher-led, simplified, whole class investigations only.

Time Required

2–3 hours

Materials Required for Main Activity

- Clear jars or glasses
- Flashlights
- Prisms
- Protractors
- Food coloring
- Small, clear containers (e.g., plastic medicine cups)
- Tempera paints
- Cardboard
- String or twine
- White construction paper
- Plastic hand lenses
- Tape
- Paper clips
- Metersticks

Materials Required for Going Further

- Incandescent and fluorescent light sources
- Paint
- Paper

Connecting to the Standards

NSES
Grades K–4 Content Standards:
Standard A: Science as Inquiry

- Abilities necessary to do scientific inquiry (especially making good observations, using data to construct a good explanation, and communicating their ideas)

- Understanding about scientific inquiry (especially developing explanations using good evidence)

Standard B: Physical Science

- Light, heat, electricity, and magnetism (especially that light can be reflected, refracted, and absorbed)

Standard C: Life Science

- Characteristics of organisms (especially that animals have specialized structures for seeing)

NCTM
Standards for Grades 3–5:

- Numbers and Operations (especially understanding and using numbers and operations)

- Measurement (especially understanding units and processes of measurement and measurable aspects of objects)

- Problem Solving (especially constructing new math knowledge through problem solving)

- Connections (especially noting the valuable interconnections between mathematics, science, and art)

Safety Considerations
Basic classroom safety practices apply.

Activity Objectives
In the following activity, students

- recognize primary and secondary colors, blend them to create new colors, and explain how they did so; and

- mix colors by spinning a multicolored disk and explain their predictions for the blended colors that result.

EXAMINING COLORS, COLOR PERCEPTION, AND SIGHT

Main Activity, Step-by-Step Procedures

1a. Before students start exploring color perception, they need to learn about several other phenomena related to light. Divide students into groups and give each group a clear glass or jar, half full of water. Instruct them to place a pencil or ruler into the water (see Figure 17.1), look at the pencil or ruler from all sides, and report on their observations. Students will notice that the pencil appears broken or bent as it enters the water. This is because the light rays (which are bouncing off the pencil and into our eyes, allowing us to see it) move faster in air than in water. Light moves at 186,000 miles per second (300,000 km/sec) in air and only at about three-fourths that speed in water (try calculating light's speed in water in terms of km/sec). That is, the light rays bouncing off the pencil are slowed down by the water and appear to bend. This phenomenon is known as *refraction*. Ask students where they have seen other instances of refraction.

FIGURE 17.1.
Refraction

Students should also understand that what they see when they view any object or color is actually the light that is being reflected by that object or color. A yellow pencil, for instance, absorbs all colors other than yellow, so that the color that reaches us, and what we perceive, is yellow.

1b. Darken the room and shine a flashlight through a prism, a beaker of water, or a crystal. Ask students what they see— on the floor, ceiling, or wall. The light passing through the prism, beaker of water, or crystal should create a rainbow, or color spectrum. Ask students to think of other times when they have seen rainbows or color spectra (maybe after a rain, on a soap bubble, or on the surface of an oily puddle). Explain to students that white light is made up of all the various colors: red, orange, yellow, green, blue, indigo, and violet. (An easy way to remember the colors in order is to recall the name ROY G. BIV.) When the white light passes through the prism, beaker, or crystal, it is refracted (bent). The various colors are refracted differently—violet is bent the most and red the least. Therefore, the colors are slightly separated when the light emerges from the prism, and we see a color spectrum. If you have enough prisms, beakers, or crystals, you

STANDARDS

SCIENCE
Abilities necessary to do
scientific inquiry

MATH
Numbers and operations
Measurement

can let each group of students create and observe spectra of their own. As they explore, challenge students to find the angle (using a protractor to measure the angles and a white sheet of paper for a "rainbow projection screen") at which the light leaves the prism (see Figure 17.2). Ask students, "How can such an angle be predicted? At what angles do the various colors travel when they leave the prism? Which colors are bent the least? Which colors are bent the most? How do you know?"

FIGURE 17.2. Spectrum

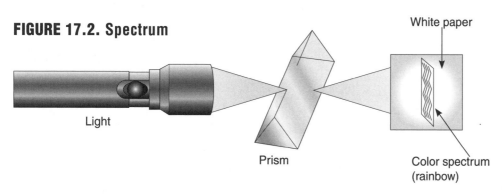

2a. Next, students can try some color mixing, using water tinted with food coloring. Each group of two or three students will need an eyedropper; several small, clear containers (e.g., plastic medicine cups); a larger container of clear water for rinsing the droppers as you explore; small containers of blue, yellow, and red (the primary colors) water; and some paper towels. Explain that students can use the eyedropper to mix different proportions of the primary colors in the medicine cups. By experimenting and exploring, the groups should be able to make other colors, such as green, orange, and violet (secondary colors). During this investigation, simply move around the room and facilitate safe and creative discovery.

Students should keep records of their experiments, so that after having sufficient time to discover, each group can report to the class about their experiences. What did students learn from their explorations? As they report their results, gently guide the discussion into the realm of specific concepts, which may include primary colors, secondary colors (green, orange, purple), the color wheel (the primary and secondary colors in a circular formation; see Figure 17.3, p. 158), value (the relative lightness or darkness of a color), and hue (gradation of color).

STANDARDS

SCIENCE
Understanding about
  scientific inquiry

MATH
Problem solving
Connections

2b. Students apply what they have learned about color mixing. Assign students one or more of the following activities, depending on their age and abilities:

- Have students create and name a new color; develop a "recipe" for the color (ask them to write down how many drops of each color they used); and make the recipe several times so that it is clearly replicable.

- Challenge students to match a teacher-created unknown color, again keeping a record of unsuccessful and successful experiments.

- Ask students to mix specific ratios of the primary colors (such as 2:1 red to yellow versus 3:1 red to yellow), record the results of any color changes due to the mixing, and look for patterns in the data. For example, do certain colors, when mixed, always produce a particular result?

- Similarly, ask students to mix specific percentages of primary colors, such as 50% blue and 50% red versus 30% blue and 70% red, again making sure to record results and watch for patterns. Hold a class discussion to find out what the groups learned, and display particularly attractive, interesting, and innovative mixtures.

3. Now that students are familiar with color mixing, they can mix colors by other methods. Using tempera paints, students paint one side of a cardboard disk one primary color and the other side another primary color. Students then make holes on opposite sides of the disk, attach strings, and, while holding a string in each hand, turn the disk repeatedly, thus winding it up. Then, they gently pull on the strings, causing the disk to spin (as in Figure 17.4). For variety, each student group should work on a different color combination. Make sure that all students predict what colors will appear when the disks are spun and that they compare the predicted colors with the actual

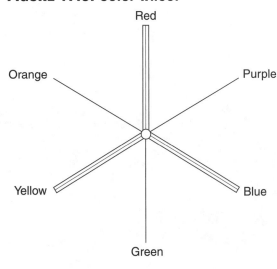

FIGURE 17.3. Color wheel

FIGURE 17.4. Spinning disk

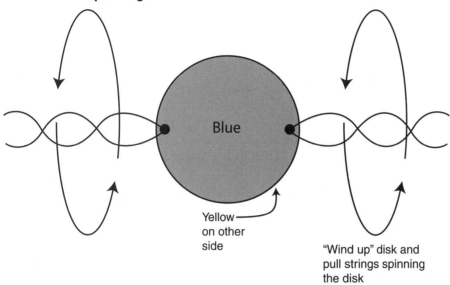

Blue

Yellow
on other
side

"Wind up" disk and
pull strings spinning
the disk

colors observed. Explain to students that the eye and brain mix the
two colors because the disk spins too rapidly for the eye to distinguish between them. The eye continues to see each color, briefly,
even as it spins out of sight. Thus, the eye tells the brain that it is
seeing a mixture of colors.

4. To expand on this activity, have student groups paint the disks with
different color ratios, proportions, or percentages and record their
results. For example, students can paint one side of a disk with a
1:1 ratio of red to blue and the other side with a 1:1 ratio of blue
to purple. Or, they can paint one side of the disk 60% red and 40%
orange and the other side 30% blue and 70% green. Be sure that
students record the colors used and their predictions. Obviously
there are an infinite number of combinations. Assist students in
noticing patterns in the data regarding what colors appear when the
disks are spun. Ask students, "What happens when primary colors are mixed? When secondary colors are mixed? When primary
colors are mixed with secondary colors? Do any particular hues
predominate? Were any surprises noted? How does math help us
design our color experiments?"

A slightly different type of spinning color disk can be made by
painting a piece of cardboard in alternating colors and threading
a string through two holes near the center (see Figure 17.5, p. 160).
By winding up and spinning the disk, the colors will mix. Again,
students can vary the ratio, proportion, or percentage of the colors

STANDARDS

SCIENCE
Characteristics of
organisms

MATH
Measurement

FIGURE 17.5.
Another spinning disk

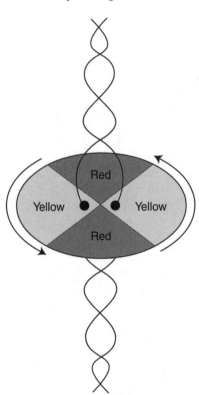

on the disk and note the perceived results. Ask students, "Which sort of disk mixed the colors best? How do you know?"

5. The human eye, or any vertebrate eye for that matter, is a very complex and amazing organ. For the next activity, students will learn more about how the eye is constructed and how it works.

Explain to students that the eye itself is an anatomical structure (see Figure 17.6). Light enters the eye through a hole called the *pupil*, which is protected by the clear cornea. The pupil is surrounded by the colored part of the eye, the *iris*, which adjusts the size of the pupil by growing larger or smaller. (The teacher can safely demonstrate this by carefully shining a flashlight into his or her eye and allowing the students to observe the changes in the pupil and iris. The pupil shrinks, which means the iris expands, in bright light to control the amount of light entering the eye. The opposite effect can be noted in dim light. Enlargement of the pupils is called *dilation*, and shrinkage is called *contraction*.) The image passes through the lens and is focused by muscles that attach to the margins of the lens and control its shape. The image then falls onto the back surface of the eye, called the *retina*, producing a chemical message that transmits the image as a nerve impulse to the

FIGURE 17.6.
The human eye (cross section)

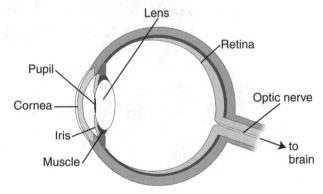

visual part of the brain via the optic nerve. The eyes, therefore, are really extensions of the brain and as such are considered part of the nervous system.

To help students learn how images form on the retina, have each group of students create a model of the eye by first cutting a 2 cm diameter hole in the center of a 15 cm × 60 cm piece of white construction paper (the hole acts as the pupil of the eye). Have students tape a plastic hand lens over the hole, and attach the two loose ends of the paper strip together using paper clips. In a darkened room, leave one window or door open and ask students to aim the "eye" at the lighted area. An inverted image should form on what would be the retina, that is, the back of the inside of the eye model (see Figure 17.7). To get a focused image, students may need to adjust the circumference of the "eye," securing it again with the paper clips. Students will see that the retinal image is in fact upside down (the brain automatically re-inverts the image, making it appear right side up) and that the shape of the eye affects one's ability to focus (accounting for far- and near-sightedness). Have students measure the optimal focal length (distance between the lens and the retina) of the eye model using a meterstick. Compare class data. Ask, "How would this compare with the focal length of an actual human eye?" Students should realize that the actual focal length is much smaller than the focal length of this large model.

FIGURE 17.7. Eye model

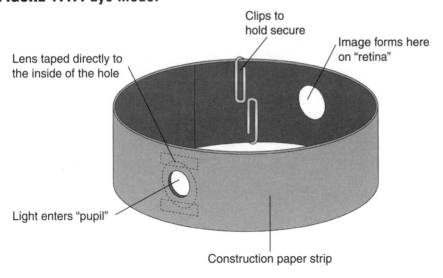

Clips to
hold secure

Image forms here
on "retina"

Lens taped directly to
the inside of the hole

Light enters "pupil"

Construction paper strip

Discussion Questions

Ask students the following:

1. What did you enjoy about mixing colors (either with colored water or with painted disks)? What surprised you about the composition of colors? What else do you want to know about colors and their composition? How could you find out?

2. What does mathematics have to do with the study of light and color? That is, how can mathematics help us understand those subjects?

3. Can you think of any art projects that would include the mixing of colors using either the spinning disks or the spinning top?

4. What sorts of variables can affect color perception? How do you know?

5. How does the human eye form an image? How do you know?

Assessment

Suggestions for specific ways to assess student understanding are provided in parentheses.

1. Did students recognize the primary and secondary colors and the organization of those hues on the color wheel? Did they create new colors, and were they able to explain how they did so? (Use observational, embedded evidence from Procedure 2 as performance assessment. Also, use Discussion Question 1 as a prompt for a science journal entry.)

2. Could students successfully mix colors by spinning a multicolored disk? Could they explain how the colors "magically" blended? (Use observational, embedded evidence from Procedure 3 as performance assessment. Also, use Discussion Question 3 as a prompt for a science journal entry.)

3. Were students able to successfully predict which colors would be produced after painting the disks with different color ratios, proportions, or percentages? (Make embedded observations during Procedure 4, and use Discussion Question 2 as a prompt for a science journal entry.)

4. Were students able to discuss the basic structure and function of a human eye? (Make embedded observations during Procedure 5, and use Discussion Question 5 as a prompt for a science journal entry.)

RUBRIC 17.1
Sample rubric using these assessment options

	Achievement Level		
	Developing 1	Proficient 2	Exemplary 3
Did students recognize the primary and secondary colors and the organization of those hues on the color wheel? Did they create new colors, and were they able to explain how they did so?	Mixed colors but were unable to adequately explain their rationales and outcomes or to adequately explain the organization of the color wheel	Successfully recognized primary colors, secondary colors, and the organization of the color wheel and adequately explained the creation of new colors	Successfully recognized primary colors, secondary colors, and the organization of the color wheel and demonstrated a deep understanding of what those concepts had to do with their own color mixing
Could students successfully mix colors by spinning a multicolored disk? Could they explain how the colors blended?	Mixed the colors by spinning but could not explain how or why the colors blended	Successfully mixed the colors by spinning and explained how the colors blended	Successfully mixed the colors by spinning and explained how the colors blended, drawing upon experiences, concepts, and terms from the preceding explorations
Were students able to successfully predict which colors would be produced after painting the disks with different color ratios, proportions, or percentages?	Constructed and spun the disks but were unable to predict which colors would appear when spun	Successfully predicted which colors would be produced when disks were painted and spun	Successfully predicted which colors would be produced and explained how the colors blended, drawing upon concepts and terms (from both science and math)
Were students able to discuss the structure and function of a human eye?	Unable to discuss the human eye to any significant extent	Successfully explained the basic structure and function of the human eye	Successfully explained the basic structure and function of the human eye, and related that discussion to their investigations of color perception

Going Further

Artists must consider many variables when producing and displaying their work, because color perception varies based on the environment and the viewer.

For instance, an individual's color perception can depend on the ambient light available. Have students look at a painted surface (one side of one of the disks painted in the main activity will do) under three different lighting sources: incandescent light (a typical lightbulb), fluorescent light, and sunlight. In each case, have students write a brief description of the color as they perceive it. This would be an opportune time to introduce several terms related to color: *hue* (the distinct colors on the color wheel, such as blue, green, violet), *intensity* (brightness and purity of color; the colors of the spectrum are high-intensity hues, and dull, neutral hues are of low intensity), and *value* (the relative lightness or darkness of a color, i.e., luminosity, which may be described as light, medium, or dark). Students may find these terms useful as they describe their color observations. Ask students, "How do your perceptions of the colors vary in different types of light? Do you notice any patterns in your results? For instance, how do intensity and value vary in the three types of light, if they vary at all?"

Another way that color perception can vary is in contrast to other colors. You can demonstrate this by placing various hues of painted surfaces next to each other. Compare the way a blue surface looks next to a yellow surface with the way it looks next to an orange, green, or red surface. For example, the boundary between blue and yellow tends to look washed out. Students can explore a variety of color combinations (again, the painted disks will be fine, or you might paint index cards in varying hues) and record their observations. Color contrast is used by painters to evoke certain reactions in the viewer. Ask students to compare the muted and balanced *Mona Lisa* by da Vinci to any of the brightly colored Fauvist works, such as those of Matisse or Derain.

Finally, color perception varies with the viewer's mental context, expectations, and assumptions. Paint a simple illustration of an apple and a tree, both of the same shade of gray paint. Mount them separately on pieces of white paper, and survey the class to see if students believe that the two paintings are the same color. Many viewers will find the apple to be more reddish and the tree to be more greenish. Students may conduct their own surveys by making their own apples and trees and taking them home to ask family members what they see.

Other Options and Extensions

1. Students might be interested to know that different cultures break up the continuous color spectrum into different colors; that is, different cultures see the "natural" breaks between colors in different places, perhaps grouping what we might call red and orange into a single color category. Interested students can find more information on this phenomenon by looking in the library or on the internet.

2. Dissect a vertebrate eye (obtain a cow, sheep, or pig eye from a butcher or from a science supply catalog), showing students the important anatomical features and tracing the path of light as it moves through the eye to become an image in the brain.

3. Have each student paint a picture, and then reproduce the same composition again, this time using entirely different colors. Encourage the use of "unnatural" colors (e.g., red trees and green skies) in the second painting. Then ask students to compare the two paintings for impact, meaning, and aesthetics. Hold a class discussion about the importance of color in paintings, using the student art as evidence (perhaps also referring to reproductions of famous works by Impressionists, Fauvists, and so forth), and attempt to notice regularities and patterns in color perception and interpretation.

Resources

Ashbrook, P. 2008. Color investigations. *Science and Children* 46 (2): 14–15.

Dalby, D. K. 1991. Fine tune your sense of color. *Science and Children* 29 (3): 24–26.

DeVita, C., and S. Ruppert. 2007. Secret message science goggles. *Science and Children* 44 (7): 30–35.

Engels, C. J. 1985. Chasing rainbows. *Science and Children* 22 (6): 13–14.

Matkins, J. J., and J. McDonnough. 2004. Circus light. *Science and Children* 41 (5): 50–54.

Ostwald, T. 1995. An eye for learning. *Science and Children* 33 (2): 25–26.

Rommel-Esham, K. 2005. Do you see what I see? *Science and Children* 43 (1): 40–43.

Sands, N. L. 1991. A splash of color. *Science and Children* 28 (6): 38–39.

Yang, D. 2006. Developing number sense through real-life situations. *Teaching Children Mathematics* 13 (2): 104–106.

+Life Science

Activity 18
Exploring the Mysteries of Fingerprints

Overview

This activity combines a variety of processes and skills into an investigation of something near and dear to your students—their fingers. Math and science blend seamlessly as students observe, compare, and apply their ideas about fingerprints.

Processes/Skills

- Observing
- Classifying
- Comparing
- Describing
- Recognizing shapes and patterns
- Predicting
- Collecting data
- Graphing
- Experimenting
- Communicating

Recommended For

Grades 2–4: Individual and small group instruction
To adapt the lesson for grade 2 students, perform Procedures 2 and 4 as teacher-led, whole class demonstrations, simplifying the process and analysis as needed.

Time Required

2–4 hours

Materials Required for Main Activity

- Smooth, nonlatex, kitchen work gloves
- A coin
- Paper
- Soft lead pencils
- Transparent tape
- Hand lenses
- Loop, whorl, and arch transparencies for projector or scanned into computer
- Extra-fine graphite powder (available at hardware store)
- Clear packing tape
- Soft-bristled brushes

Materials Required for Going Further

- Sponges
- Tempera paints
- Stamp pads
- Baby powder
- Flour
- Talcum powder
- Baking powder

Connecting to the Standards

NSES
Grades K–4 Content Standards:
Standard A: Science as Inquiry

- Abilities necessary to do scientific inquiry (especially making good observations, using data to construct a good explanation, and communicating their ideas)
- Understanding about scientific inquiry (especially developing explanations using good evidence)

Standard C: Life Science

- Characteristics of organisms (each animal has different structures, in this case, fingerprints, that serve in survival)

NCTM
Standards for Grades PreK–2, 3–5:

- Algebra (especially recognizing and describing patterns)

- Problem Solving (especially constructing new math knowledge through problem solving)

- Reasoning and Proof (especially developing, selecting, and evaluating arguments and proofs)

- Connections (especially noting the valuable interconnections between mathematics, science, and art)

- Representation (especially using graphic representations to model phenomena and solve problems)

Safety Considerations

Basic classroom safety practices apply.

Activity Objectives

In the following activity, students

- identify and classify their fingerprints based on shape;

- count and graphically portray their findings; and

- collect fingerprints from around the classroom after predicting likely locations.

Main Activity, Step-by-Step Procedures

1. Ask students to look closely at the palm side of their fingers. What do they notice? Do they see the tiny ridges that form the finger-prints? What do they know about fingerprints? What would they like to know? How could they find answers to their questions? How do fingerprints benefit us? (For a quick answer, they should try picking up a dime while wearing smooth, nonlatex gloves.) Students might respond that fingerprints help our fingers grab onto things by providing friction.

SCIENCE
Abilities necessary to do scientific inquiry

MATH
Problem solving

EXPLORING THE MYSTERIES OF FINGERPRINTS

SCIENCE
Characteristics of
organisms

MATH
Algebra
Representation

SCIENCE
Understanding about
scientific inquiry

MATH
Reasoning and proof

MATH
Connections

2. Ask students, "Are your fingerprints the same on all of your fingers? How could we get a better look at your prints?" Ask students to rub the lead of a soft pencil on a piece of scratch paper and then rub one of their fingers in the pencil lead so that their fingertip picks up some of the coloring (like a rubber stamp on an ink pad). Next, students take a small piece of transparent adhesive tape and stick it over the fingertip covered with pencil lead. If they gently press the tape on the finger, some of the lead will be transferred to the tape. Tell students to stick the tape to a piece of white paper. They should be able to see their fingerprint, outlined in pencil lead, through the tape. Students should make copies of all 10 fingerprints this way, making sure to label each tape-print with the correct finger (for example, "right index finger"—see Activity Sheet 18.1, p. 177). Ask students, "Are your prints the same on all of your fingers? How are they different? How are they similar?" A hand lens may be useful here.

3. In small groups, students can compare their own print sets to those of other students. They should look for similarities and patterns. Ask students, "How many categories of prints do you see? How would you describe the categories that you see? Looking at the prints from the entire class, how many categories, based on shapes, can you identify?" Ask the class to count the number of students in each fingerprint category and, with their help, make a bar graph of the class results on the chalkboard.

4. Introduce the notion of the three basic fingerprint shapes—loop, whorl, and arch (see Figure 18.1). Ask students, "How do these categories compare to the categories named by the class?" Have students count the number of people in class with loop, whorl, and arch prints, and make another bar graph of those results. Ask students, "In your class, which shape is most common? Least common? Are all loops the same? All whorls? All arches? Explain."

5. Next, students can use what they've learned to identify unknown prints. Have each student make two tape-prints of the same finger (the index finger of the right hand, for instance). Have students keep one print, write their names on the back, and leave them out on their desks. They hand the other print to you as you come around the classroom. Secretly keep track of the actual owners of these tape-prints, as these will be the fingerprint "unknowns." (You can use numbers from the roll sheet, so no names appear on the paper; only you should know who each print belongs to.) Have students work in pairs or small groups, and give each work group an

FIGURE 18.1. Fingerprints

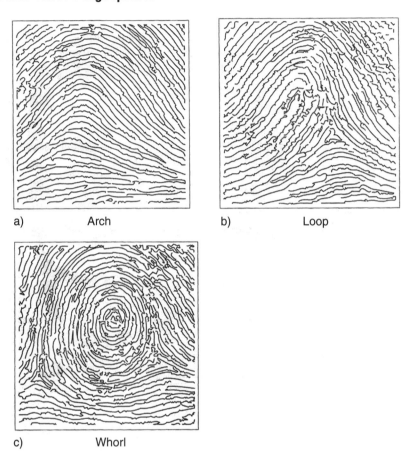

a)   Arch   b)   Loop

c)   Whorl

unknown tape-print. Also make hand lenses available. Ask students how they might identify the owner of the unknown fingerprints: "What would you look for? How could you differentiate between two similar prints? What sorts of careers might involve activities such as this?" Challenge them to compare the unknown print with the known prints (the set the students left out on their desks) and identify the owners. When all have completed the task, ask how they went about comparing and identifying. Ask, "Which groups were successful and why? Which techniques or strategies worked and which didn't?" Tell students to keep the first set of prints (those marked with names) for the following activity.

6. Tell students to imagine that a crime has been committed in the classroom and that they need to identify the culprits by locating their fingerprints. Have the class predict where in the classroom they would expect to find lots of fingerprints. Also, where would they expect to find only a few prints? Have them explain their predictions. Using extra-fine graphite powder (a lubricant available in hardware stores) and wide pieces of clear, adhesive tape (packing tape works well for this), send groups around the classroom to collect quantities of fingerprints.

To collect prints, students lightly dust the identified area with graphite powder. They then gently dust away the excess powder with soft-bristled brushes and lightly press pieces of tape onto the dusted area. Next, they press the tape onto white paper, labeling the paper with the location from which the prints were lifted and the investigators' names. Ask students to predict the places where prints are likely to be found (perhaps doorknobs, desktops, or the handle of a pencil sharpener, for example), then check for prints. Results would support the predictions if prints are common in these places. Students should also predict and check the places unlikely to have prints; results would falsify the predictions if prints were common in these locations. Students should then compare their results, looking for patterns in the evidence. Ask students to make a bar graph of prints per location using the class results. Discuss the relationship of fingerprint presence to classroom activity. Ask students, "Where were prints not found? What surfaces would be unlikely to 'hold' clear prints? What surfaces hold prints well?" (For example, rough or porous surfaces are unlikely to have many prints, while smooth, hard surfaces tend to have many prints.) Have students attempt to identify some of the lifted prints using the known set from Procedure 5. Ask students, "What factors influence an investigator's ability to identify fingerprints? If you were a detective investigating a burglary in someone's home, where would you first dust for fingerprints? Why? In what other jobs would fingerprinting and fingerprints be useful? How could fingerprinting be useful in your day-to-day life?"

Discussion Questions

Ask students the following:

1. Can you think of any other ways to make a set of fingerprints? Explain.

2. How were you able to tell one person's prints from another's? What specific techniques did you use to identify them?

3. What do your observations and results from these activities tell you about fingerprints? About fingers?

Assessment

Suggestions for specific ways to assess student understanding are provided in parentheses.

1. Were students able to identify patterns in their own fingerprints and see similarities between their prints and the prints of others? (Use observational, embedded evidence from Procedures 2 and 3 as performance assessment. Also, use Discussion Question 2 as a prompt for a science journal entry.)

2. Were students able to identify loop, arch, and whorl prints? Could they graphically portray the classroom frequencies of these three categories? (Use observational, embedded evidence from Procedures 3 and 4 as performance assessment.)

3. Were students able to accurately identify the bearers of unknown prints? (Use observational, embedded evidence from Procedure 5 as performance assessment. Use Discussion Question 2 as a prompt for a science journal entry.)

4. Were students able to effectively locate and lift prints from various locations in the classroom or school? (Use observational, embedded evidence from Procedure 6 as performance assessment.)

5. Could students see the value of fingerprints in various jobs (e.g., detectives) and possibly in their everyday lives? (Use observations from all the procedures, Procedure 3 as embedded assessment, and Discussion Question 3 as a prompt for a science journal entry.)

RUBRIC 18.1
Sample rubric using these assessment options

	Achievement Level		
	Developing 1	Proficient 2	Exemplary 3
Were students able to identify patterns in their own fingerprints and see similarities between their prints and the prints of others?	Attempted, but were unable to successfully identify patterns or see similarities	Successfully identified patterns and recognized similarities	Successfully identified patterns and recognized similarities, and discussed the experiences using appropriate concepts and terms
Were students able to identify loop, arch, and whorl prints? Could they graphically portray the classroom frequencies of these three categories?	Attempted but were unable to successfully identify loop, arch, and/or whorl	Successfully identified all three types of fingerprints in self and others	Successfully identified all three types of fingerprints in self and others, and graphically portrayed the classroom frequencies
Were students able to accurately identify the bearers of unknown prints?	Attempted, but were unable to successfully identify unknowns	Successfully identified unknown fingerprints	Successfully identified unknown fingerprints, and discussed the experiences using appropriate concepts and terms

Going Further

Students can make paintings using their finger and thumb prints (maybe even footprints) as "printing stamps" (see Figure 18.2). Use tempera paint on wet sponges, dry tempera paint on sponge-moistened fingers, finger paints, or even ink from stamp pads. You may want to experiment with other color sources or try various colors and weights of paper. Some students might want to make this project into a collage, a mosaic, or a mobile. Encourage creativity, experimentation, and playfulness.

Other Options and Extensions

1. Have students replicate the basic activities, but instead of making fingerprints have them make toe prints. Ask, "How do the results compare with fingerprints?"

2. Are fingerprints genetically inherited traits? Have students collect the prints of family members and compare class results.

3. Challenge students: "What forms the fingerprint? How do you know? Can you discover ways to keep from leaving prints without covering your fingers with gloves? How can you make heavier prints?"

FIGURE 18.2. Fingerprint painting

4. Encourage students to make prints of other areas of skin, such as the elbow, knee, back of the hand, and so on, and compare those prints with their fingerprints.

5. To make Procedure 6 more inquiry-based, have students try to pick up prints using a variety of substances such as baby powder, flour, talcum powder, and baking powder. Before they use the substances to pick up prints, ask them to make predictions about which substances will work, which won't, and why or why not. Students may also explore the feasibility of lifting prints from different surfaces (e.g., smooth, rough, or porous surfaces). Ask students, "What types of surfaces are best or worst for picking up prints, and how do you explain your results?"

6. Encourage students to find out what the terms *criminology* and *forensics* mean. Ask, "What sorts of jobs might involve activities such as fingerprinting? Are there any other aspects of criminology or forensics that interest you?"

7. Another possibility is for students to create a large fractal finger-print. A *fractal* is a shape made up of smaller, identical versions of itself. This "fingerprint fractal" can be created by forming small prints into the shape of one giant print. Ask students to make a painting of a giant print, a loop shape for instance, made up entirely of their fingerprint "stamps." This mural-like giant print could be a group project.

Resources

Beisel, R. W., and J. Hechtman. 1989. Sleuthing is elementary. *Science and Children* 26 (8): 17–19.

Gillespie, D. C. 1984. Science at your fingerprints. *Science and Children* 22 (1): 8–10.

Soares, J., M. L. Blanton, and J. J. Kaput. 2006. Thinking algebraically across the elementary school curriculum. *Teaching Children Mathematics* 12 (5): 228–235.

Solomon, A. C. 1978. Fingerprints. *Science and Children* 15 (4): 30.

Twiest, M. M. 1986. Skin prints. *Science and Children* 23 (8): 26–27.

ACTIVITY SHEET 18.1
Exploring the Mysteries of Fingerprints

1. What I know about fingerprints:

2. What I want to know about fingerprints:

3. Collect your fingerprints here:

	Thumb	Index Finger	Middle Finger	Ring Finger	Little Finger
Right Hand					
Left Hand					

4. What conclusions can you draw about the shapes of your own fingerprints?

5. What patterns can you identify when you compare your prints to those of your classmates?

6. On a separate piece of paper or the back of this sheet, make a bar graph of the number of students in each fingerprint category (arch, loop, whorl).

7. What I learned about fingerprints:

Activity **19**

Making Prints From Fruits and Vegetables

Overview

Students may be familiar with eating fruits and vegetables, but have they ever taken a really close look at the anatomy of those specimens? In this activity, students have an opportunity to explore aspects of the internal and external anatomy of produce by making prints of fruits and vegetables. As students discover the fun of printmaking, they observe and compare botanical shapes, patterns, and textures in the resulting prints. By adding or limiting the degree and complexity of concept introduction, altering the required amount of student tool use, and modifying questioning techniques, this activity is easily adapted to all grades in the K–4 range.

Processes/Skills

- Observing
- Counting
- Predicting
- Describing
- Inferring from data
- Inquiring
- Communicating
- Printing
- Recognizing shapes and patterns
- Problem solving

Recommended For

Grades K–4: Small group instruction
To adapt the lesson for students in grades K–1 you'll want to forego student

use of plastic knives in Procedure 3. Also, offer plenty of assistance during the printmaking process in Procedures 4 and 5.

Time Required
1–3 hours

Materials Required for Main Activity

- An assortment of fresh produce (see sample list in Procedure 1)
- A sharp knife (for teacher use only)
- Plastic knives (for older student use only)
- Paper
- Newspaper
- Tempera paints in a variety of colors
- A means of inking the stamps (e.g., brushes, sponges, cloths, plastic dishes, paper towels, small brayers [paint rollers])

Connecting to the Standards

NSES
Grades K–4 Content Standards:
Standard A: Science as Inquiry

- Abilities necessary to do scientific inquiry (especially making good observations, using data to construct a good explanation, and communicating their ideas)
- Understanding about scientific inquiry (especially developing explanations using good evidence)

Standard C: Life Science

- Characteristics of organisms (each plant has different structures that serve in growth, survival, and reproduction)

NCTM
Standards for Grades PreK–2, 3–5:

- Numbers and Operations (especially understanding and using numbers, operations, and estimating)
- Algebra (especially recognizing and describing patterns)

- Geometry (especially identifying, naming, and/or comparing two- and three-dimensional shapes)

- Problem Solving (especially constructing new math knowledge through problem solving)

- Connections (especially noting the valuable interconnections between mathematics, science, and art)

Safety Considerations

Basic classroom safety practices apply. Be sure that the sharp knife is for teacher use *only*. Instruct students in proper, safe use of the plastic knives, as well. Check ahead of time for any food allergies, and be particularly cautious with peppers (you might want to use them only for demonstration purposes).

Activity Objectives

In the following activity, students

- make, observe, and analyze prints from a variety of fruit and vegetable specimens; and

- identify geometric shapes, numbers, and numeric patterns within the fruits and vegetables by observing the prints that they make.

Main Activity, Step-by-Step Procedures

1. Collect an assortment of fruits and vegetables, such as apples, oranges, mushrooms, carrots, lemons, cucumbers, onions, potatoes, peppers, turnips, celery, lettuce and cabbage leaves, tomatoes, garlic, bananas, squash, grapes, and snow peas. You can encourage diversity and involvement by requesting that students each bring in at least one piece of produce themselves. Ask students to identify the various fruits and vegetables and to describe the inner structure of each. For each example, ask, "What part of the plant is this and what job does it do for the plant?" For younger students, encourage student observation by counting out the parts of the various specimens (such as sides of a banana, eyes of a potato, or seeds in a grape). Also, encourage students to look for repeating patterns within the specimen's structure (such as layers in the onion or sections in the orange). This would be an opportune time to introduce the terms *botany* and *anatomy*. Explain to students that these specimens will be used to make prints, and ask the class to suggest ways

SCIENCE
Characteristics of
organisms

SCIENCE
Abilities necessary to do
  scientific inquiry

MATH
Algebra

SCIENCE
Understanding about
  scientific inquiry

MATH
Numbers and operations
Problem solving

MATH
Connections

to make prints from the fruits and vegetables. Demonstrate how to make a basic print, using either the outside or the inside of the specimen. Ask, "What do you think we might see if we make prints of these fruits and vegetables?"

2. Ask students for predictions. "Which fruits or vegetables will make good prints? Which will not? Why or why not? What qualities make a 'good' print?"

3. With a sharp knife, cut the harder produce into various sections (do not allow students to do this; only you should use the sharp knife). For the softer specimens, allow students to make their own cuts with plastic knives. Tell students to cut the specimens in a variety of directions—cross sections (cut in half through the short axis of the specimen), longitudinal sections (cut in half through the long axis of the specimen), at different angles, in halves, and in quarters. Keep produce such as cabbage leaves intact because students will make prints of the entire specimen.

4. Allow students to experiment with the various shapes and print technique possibilities. Instruct students to pay attention to texture, shape, and pattern within each fruit or vegetable print. Demonstrate what you mean by "texture, shape, and pattern" with an example or two.

5. Provide plenty of paper for this project. For clearer printing (and easier cleanup), cushion the stamped paper with several underlying layers of newspaper. Students can ink the stamps in any of three ways: (a) apply paint (tempera) directly to the specimen using a brush; (b) make a stamp pad by placing a sponge, folded cloth, or paper towel in a shallow dish or lid and saturating it with thick tempera paint; or (c) spread paint on larger specimens with a brayer (a small paint roller, available at arts or crafts stores). Offer students a variety of tempera paint colors.

6. Encourage students to identify shapes in their prints (e.g., lines, circles, rectangles), numbers (e.g., number of seeds visible in the split apple), or patterns (starlike arrangement of the core of the split apple). Students can even outline or otherwise mark shapes, numbers, or patterns observed in the dried print with charcoal, chalk, or pencil.

7. Display examples of student prints on the bulletin board. Discuss as a class or in small groups the variety of printing techniques; artistic results; and anatomical, structural, and mathematical observations.

Discussion Questions

Ask students the following:

1. What did you notice about the various fruits and vegetables regarding their inner or outer texture, anatomy, form, or structure?

2. What geometric shapes, numbers, and numeric patterns did you find in the fruits or vegetables? What shapes, numbers, or patterns are most common? Least common? How do you know that they are most or least common?

3. What surprised you about this activity? Why?

4. When it comes to printmaking, the part I like best is _____. (Encourage students to write their answers to this last question in their science journals.)

Assessment

Suggestions for specific ways to assess student understanding are provided in parentheses.

1. Were students able to successfully make prints from the various specimens? (Use observational, embedded evidence from Procedures 4 and 5 as performance assessment. Also, use Discussion Question 4 as a prompt for a science journal entry.)

2. Were students able to identify regularities or abnormalities in internal and external texture, anatomy, and overall structure in these botanical specimens? Could they explain something about the diversity of botanical structure? (Make embedded observations during Procedure 6, and use Discussion Question 2 as a prompt for a science journal entry.)

3. Did students identify geometric shapes, numbers, and numeric patterns in their fruit and vegetable prints? (Use observational, embedded evidence from Procedures 6 and 7 as performance assessment.)

RUBRIC 19.1
Sample rubric using these assessment options

	Achievement Level		
	Developing 1	**Proficient** 2	**Exemplary** 3
Were students able to successfully make prints from the various specimens?	Attempted but were unsuccessful in making clear prints from the specimens	Successfully made clear prints from several specimens	Successfully made clear prints from a wide variety of specimens and were able to explain the printmaking process
Were students able to identify regularities or abnormalities in internal and external texture, anatomy, and overall structure in these botanical specimens? Could they explain something about the diversity of botanical structure?	Attempted to discuss the botanical anatomy of the specimens but were unable to do so to any significant extent	Successfully identified several details of anatomical structure, and explained several generalizations about botanical structure	Successfully identified a wide variety of anatomical details, and connected those details to a variety of generalizations about botanical structure
Did students identify geometric shapes, numbers, and numeric patterns in their fruit and vegetable prints?	Attempted to identify math aspects of the prints but were unsuccessful	Successfully identified several math aspects of the prints	Successfully identified several math aspects of the prints and were able to relate them to one another and to their anatomical structure

Other Options and Extensions

1. Encourage students to further investigate the anatomical differences among fruits and vegetables through printmaking or through research at the library or on the internet.

2. Ask students to experiment with the printing method (e.g., use more, less, or different paint; different ways of inking the stamp; different types of paper).

3. Have students extend the printing process to other specimens (e.g., leaves, branches, whole fish, sponge, wood blocks, rocks, dried seaweed).

4. Ask students to make an environmental mural (e.g., rain forest, underwater, desert) using stamps.

5. Extend the mathematical component of the activity by collecting data via the prints. For example, students could measure and compute class averages of lemon diameters, lime circumferences, apple weight versus apple diameter, average number of peas in a pod, and so on. Data can be graphed, analyzed, and discussed.

6. For a social studies connection, have students examine fruits and vegetables from around the world, if available in your community, and allow students to find out how different cultures use the fruits and vegetables.

Resources

Angerame, S. S. 1999. Math-o'-lanterns. *Teaching Children Mathematics* 6 (2): 72.

Gerber, B. 1995. These plants have potential. *Science and Children* 32 (1): 32–34.

Lowry, P. K., and J. H. McCrary. 2001. Someone's in the kitchen with science. *Science and Children* 39 (2): 22–27.

Miller, J. 1973. Ozalid printing. *Science and Children* 10 (7): 35.

Mitchell, C. W. 1985. Leaf printing. *Science and Children* 23 (2): 24–26.

Yang, D. 2006. Developing number sense through real-life situations in school. *Teaching Children Mathematics* 13 (2): 104–106.

Overview

In this activity, students make *serial sections* of an apple. Students make cross-section prints of the top portion of the apple, then another print further into the apple, and so on until they get to the bottom of the apple. This serial sectioning technique provides almost a three-dimensional view of the inside of the apple and serves as a good aid in discerning the complete internal anatomy of the fruit. Students can use their newfound knowledge of fruit anatomy to label their completed serial prints.

The apple is a type of fruit known as a *pome*. A pome is defined as a fruit whose fleshy parts are all derived from the flower and enclose the portions produced by the pericarp (see Figure 20.2, p. 190). A pear is also a pome.

Processes/Skills

- Observing
- Predicting
- Describing
- Analyzing
- Concluding
- Measuring
- Calculating
- Inquiring
- Communicating
- Recognizing shapes and patterns
- Developing spatial sense
- Cooperating

Recommended For

Grades K–4: Small group instruction

When working with students in grades K–1, first ask for predictions and then slice the sections for them before assisting them with printing serial sections.

Time Required

1–2 hours

Materials Required for Main Activity

- Apples
- A sharp knife (for teacher use only) or plastic knives (for older student use only)
- Paper
- Newspaper
- Tempera paints in a variety of colors
- A means of inking the stamps (e.g., brushes, sponges, cloths, plastic dishes, paper towels, small brayers [paint rollers])

Connecting to the Standards

NSES
Grades K–4 Content Standards:

Standard A: Science as Inquiry

- Abilities necessary to do scientific inquiry (especially making good observations, using data to construct a good explanation, and communicating their ideas)

Standard C: Life Science

- Characteristics of organisms (each plant has different structures that serve in growth, survival, and reproduction)

NCTM
Standards for Grades PreK–2, 3–5:

- Numbers and Operations (especially understanding and using numbers, operations, and estimating)
- Geometry (especially identifying, naming, and/or comparing two- and three-dimensional shapes)

- Measurement (especially understanding units and processes of measurement and measurable aspects of objects)

- Connections (especially noting the valuable interconnections between mathematics, science, and art)

Safety Considerations

Basic classroom safety practices apply. Be sure that the sharp knife is for teacher use *only*. Instruct students in the proper, safe use of plastic knives.

Activity Objectives

In the following activity, students

- make prints from serial sections of an apple and explain how that series of prints provides a three-dimensional view of the inner apple; and

- observe, discuss, and compare the internal characteristics of apples, including number-related and shape-related patterns.

Main Activity, Step-by-Step Procedures

1. Begin by asking students if they have ever seen the inside of a fruit or a vegetable. When students confirm that they have, ask if they have ever seen the entire inside all at once. Not likely. X-rays allow us to see inside things, but we don't have x-ray equipment in the classroom. Explain that the students are going to create serial sections of an apple, and that a serial section is like a sliced-up loaf of bread (i.e., a series of cross sections through a single specimen). Ask students, "What would you like to know about the inside of an apple?" Note their responses on the chalkboard.

2. Assemble students into small groups, and provide each group with a whole apple. Have each group make and document predictions about what they think they'll find inside the apple. Students must then measure the length (height) of the apple, in millimeters, and decide how many slices are appropriate for the size of their particular specimen. Four to seven slices should be reasonable. With longer specimens (such as cucumbers), or with older students, more slices can be made. Once students decide on the number of cross sections to make, they must divide the entire length by the number of slices plus one (we add one because we're really dividing the length by the number of sections into which the specimen is to be cut) to determine how far apart each section must be for all sections to be of

SCIENCE
Abilities necessary to do
   scientific inquiry

MATH
Numbers and operations
Measurement

SCIENCE
Characteristics of
   organisms

EXAMINING SERIAL SECTIONS OF AN APPLE

FIGURE 20.1. Apple sections

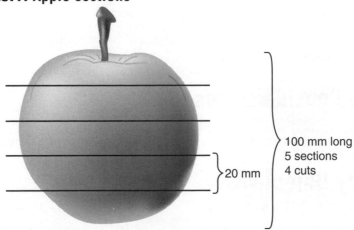

100 mm long
5 sections
4 cuts

20 mm

MATH
Geometry
Connection

equal depth. For example, a 100 mm apple with four slices will have a cut every 20 mm (see Figure 20.1).

3. The teacher can slice the apple for students with a metal knife, or older students can make the cuts themselves, using a plastic knife. In either case, each group should slice just one section at a time to keep each slice fresh and to minimize confusion. Using the same printmaking techniques outlined in Activity 19, students produce a series of internal views of their apples. When all prints are completed and the paint has dried, the views should be labeled thoroughly. Labels should include information about the specimen (type of specimen, total length, thickness of sections, any unusual characteristics of the entire specimen), the internal anatomy (basic features; see Figure 20.2), and the investigators (names and responsibilities).

FIGURE 20.2. Apple anatomy

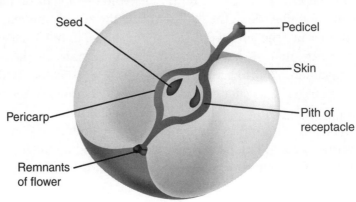

Seed

Pedicel

Skin

Pericarp

Pith of receptacle

Remnants of flower

Students can then examine their illustrations for patterns and regularities, comparing their serial views with those of other groups. What generalizations can they make about the internal anatomy of apples? Consider the shapes of the apple's parts, the location of its seeds, the size of the receptacle, the location of the pericarp, and any student questions noted earlier on the chalkboard. Have students reflect on the accuracy of their predictions. Ask, "What have you learned about the internal anatomy of the apple? What else do you want to know about fruits and vegetables?"

Discussion Questions

Ask students the following:

1. How is the set of serial views like looking at an x-ray of the apple's insides? How is it different from an x-ray?

2. What arithmetic or geometric patterns did you identify within the apple?

3. In terms of their internal anatomy, how are apples similar? How do they differ?

Assessment

Suggestions for specific ways to assess student understanding are provided in parentheses.

1. Were students able to successfully make a series of prints from serial sections of the apple? (Use observational evidence from Procedure 3 as performance assessment.)

2. Were students able to observe, discuss, and compare the internal characteristics of apples, including number-related and shape-related patterns? (Use student responses to Discussion Questions 2 and 3 as embedded assessment and as prompts for science journal entries.)

3. Did students get a sense of how the serial sections provide an x-ray or three-dimensional perspective of the inner apple? (Use student responses to Discussion Question 1 as an embedded assessment and as a prompt for a science journal entry.)

RUBRIC 20.1
Sample rubric using these assessment options

	Achievement Level		
	Developing 1	Proficient 2	Exemplary 3
Were students able to successfully make a series of prints from serial sections of the apple?	Attempted to make prints, but were unsuccessful	Successfully made serial prints	Successfully made serial prints and were able to explain the apple's anatomy using appropriate concepts and terms
Were students able to observe, discuss, and compare the internal characteristics of apples, including shape-related patterns?	Observed but were unable to discuss significant aspects of the apple's internal anatomy	Successfully observed, discussed, and compared the apple's anatomy	Successfully observed, discussed, and compared the apple's anatomy, and were able to describe several shape-related patterns
Did they get a sense of how the serial sections provide an x-ray or 3-D perspective of the inner apple?	Observed the serial section prints but were not able to discern the 3-D perspective	Successfully discerned and described the serial sections' 3-D effect	Successfully discerned and described the serial sections' 3-D effect, using appropriate concepts and terms

Other Options and Extensions

Have students investigate the anatomy of other kinds of fruits: *berries* (tomatoes, grapes, dates, avocados, and citrus fruits), *drupes* (peaches, plums, cherries, olives, and apricots), and *false berries* (cucumber, squash, banana, cantaloupe, and cranberry). Ask students to compare serial sections of other fruits with those of the apple.

The activity can be done with printmaking, as suggested, or by having students make their own pencil illustrations of the serial sections. If students make pencil illustrations, have them choose hard specimens such as peppers, apples, cucumbers, or squash, because they are more easily cut into thin sections and are much less messy (it is easier to draw them). The printmaking activity is quicker and offers more connections to the visual arts (the actual serial prints can be quite beautiful). But the illustration activity requires students to observe the cross sections more closely and tends to require less cleanup.

Resources

Angerame, S. S. 1999. Math-o'-lanterns. *Teaching Children Mathematics* 6 (2): 72.
Coffman, M., and P. Liggit. 2005. Johnny Appleseed comes to class. *Science and Children* 43 (1): 48–51.

Gerber, B. 1995. These plants have potential. *Science and Children* 33 (1): 32–34.

Jenkins, P. D. 1980. *Art for the fun of it.* New York: Fireside.

Lowry, P. K., and J. H. McCrary. 2001. Someone's in the kitchen with science. *Science and Children* 39 (2): 22–27.

Miller, J. 1973. Ozalid printing. *Science and Children* 10 (7): 35.

Yang, D. 2006. Developing number sense through real-life situations in school. *Teaching Children Mathematics* 13 (2): 104–106.

Interdisciplinary Resources

Science and Mathematics
Specific Ideas for Lesson Development

Goldston, M. J., ed. 2004. *Stepping up to science and math.* Arlington, VA: NSTA Press.

Great Explorations in Math and Science (GEMS) series. Berkeley, CA: Lawrence Hall of Science.

Kellough, R. D., J. S. Cangelosi, A. T. Collette, E. L. Chiappetta, R. J. Souviney, L. W. Trowbridge, and R. W. Bybee. 1996. *Integrating mathematics and science for intermediate and middle school grades.* Englewood Cliffs, NJ: Merrill.

Kellough, R. D., A. A. Carin, C. Seefeldt, N. Barbour, and R. J. Souviney. 1996. *Integrating mathematics and science for kindergarten and primary grades.* Englewood Cliffs, NJ: Merrill.

Lawlor, R. 1982. *Sacred geometry.* London: Thames and Hudson.

National Science Teachers Association. 2003. *Mixing it up: Integrated, interdisciplinary, intriguing science in the elementary classroom.* Arlington, VA: NSTA Press.

Project AIMS (Activities Integrating Math and Science) series. Fresno, CA: AIMS Education Foundation.

Science (or Math) and Art
Ideas for Lessons and Interdisciplinary Instruction

Churchill, E. R. 1990. *Paper science toys.* New York: Sterling.

Dubeck, L. W., S. E. Moshier, and J. E. Boss. 1988. *Science in cinema.* New York: Teachers College Press.

Kohl, M. A., and J. Potter. 1993. *Science arts.* Bellingham, WA: Bright Ring.

Nurosi, A. 2000. Colorful illusions: Tricks to fool your eyes. New York: Sterling.

Ritter, D. 1995. *Math art.* Cypress, CA: Creative Teaching Press.

Tolley, K. 1994. *The art and science connection.* Menlo Park, CA: Addison-Wesley.

Williams, D. 1995. *Teaching mathematics through children's art.* Portsmouth, NH: Heineman.

Science Process Activities
Ideas for Lessons and Interdisciplinary Instruction

Cobb, V. 1979. *More science experiments you can eat.* New York: Harper & Row.

Ingram, M. 1993. *Bottle biology.* Dubuque, IA: Kendall/Hunt.

Mandell, M. 1959. *Physics experiments for children.* New York: Dover.

Ostlund, K. L. 1992. *Science process skills.* Menlo Park, CA: Addison-Wesley.

Packard, M. 2006. *Mythbusters: Don't try this at home.* San Francisco: Jossey-Bass.

Rezba, R. J., C. Sprague, R. L. Fiel, and H. J. Funk. 1995. *Learning and assessing science process skills.* Dubuque, IA: Kendall/Hunt.

Strongin, H. 1991. *Science on a shoestring.* Menlo Park, CA: Addison-Wesley.

Tolman, M. N., and J. O. Morton. 1986. *Earth science activities for grades 2–8.* West Nyack, NY: Parker.

United Nations Educational, Scientific, and Cultural Organization. 1962. *700 science experiments for everyone.* New York: Doubleday.

Van Cleave, J. 1989. *Chemistry for every kid.* New York: Wiley.

Walpole, B. 1988. *175 science experiments.* New York: Random House.

Art Ideas and Activities
Ideas for Lessons and Interdisciplinary Instruction

Cornett, C. E. 1999. *The arts as meaning makers.* Upper Saddle River, NJ: Merrill.

Goldberg, M. 1997. *Arts and learning.* New York: Longman.

Jenkins, P. D. 1980. *Art for the fun of it.* New York: Fireside.

Olshansky, B. 1990. *Portfolio of illustrated step-by-step art projects for young children.* New York: Center for Applied Research in Education.

Stribling, M. L. 1970. *Art from found materials.* New York: Crown.

Terzian, A. M. 1993. *The kids' multicultural art book.* Charlotte, VT: Williamson.

Thompson, K. B., and D. S. Loftus. 1995. *Art connections.* Glenview, IL: Good Year Books.

Science and Science Teaching Information
Useful Background Information

Craig, A., and C. Rosney. 1988. *The Usborne science encyclopedia.* Tulsa, OK: EDC.

Ebeneezer, J. V., and E. Lau. 1999. *Science on the internet.* Upper Saddle River, NJ: Merrill.

Gabel, D. L., ed. 1994. *Handbook of research on science teaching and learning.* New York: Macmillan.

Kwan, T., and J. Texley. 2002. *Exploring safely: A guide for elementary teachers.* Arlington, VA: NSTA Press.

National Science Teachers Association. 2003. *Safety in the elementary science classroom.* Arlington, VA: NSTA Press.

Roy, K. R. 2007. *The NSTA ready-reference guide to safer science.* Arlington, VA: NSTA Press.

Tobin, K., ed. 1993. *The practice of constructivism in science education.* Washington, DC: AAAS Press.

Trefil, J. 1992. *1001 things everyone should know about science.* New York: Doubleday.

Professional Journals

Science and Children

Teaching Children Mathematics (formerly *The Arithmetic Teacher*)

School Science and Mathematics

National Standards

American Association for the Advancement of Science. 1993. *Benchmarks for science literacy.* New York: Oxford University Press.

National Council of Teachers of Mathematics. 2000. *Principles and standards for school mathematics.* Reston, VA: Author.

National Council of Teachers of Mathematics. 2006. *Curriculum focal points for prekindergarten through grade 8 mathematics.* Reston, VA: Author.

National Research Council. 1996. *National science education standards.* Washington, DC: National Academy Press.

Internet Resources

Chem4Kids: *http://chem4kids.com*
Lessons and background information in chemistry

Dragonfly: *www.units.muohio.edu/dragonfly*
Student-friendly, interactive website, including many interdisciplinary
lesson ideas for teachers

The Educator's Reference Desk: *http://ericir.syr.edu/cgi-bin/printlessons.
cgi/Virtual/Lessons/Science/SCI0025.html*
Science lesson ideas, background information, and resources for teachers

The Geometry in Space Project: *www.math-ed.com/Resources/GIS/
Geometry_In_Space*
Interactive site with interdisciplinary lesson ideas related to space travel

Houghton Mifflin Harcourt Education Place Activity Search:
http://eduplace.com/activity
Specific lesson ideas in science, math, and other disciplines

Keep America Beautiful: *www.kab.org/site/PageServer?pagename=index*
Background information and lesson ideas on recycling and waste reduction

Kids as Global Scientists: *www.biokids.umich.edu/research/kgs*
Interdisciplinary lesson ideas, background information, resources for teachers and students

KinderArt: *http://kinderart.com*
Many art lesson ideas, including interdisciplinary lessons, for young
students

National Council of Teachers of Mathematics: *www.nctm.org*
All aspects of classroom math

National Science Teachers Association: *www.nsta.org*
All aspects of classroom science

Northwest Regional Educational Laboratory (NWREL) Library in the Sky: *http://nwrel.org/sky/index.php*
Interdisciplinary lesson ideas

Science NetLinks: *http://sciencenetlinks.com*
American Association for the Advancement of Science site offering lessons, background information, and resources

Thinking Fountain: *www.thinkingfountain.org*
Many science lesson ideas, including interdisciplinary lessons

United Nations CyberSchoolBus: *http://un.org/Pubs/CyberSchoolBus*
United Nations site for human rights/social justice education, interdisciplinary lessons and background information

Why Files: *http://whyfiles.org*
Science, math, and technology news and background information

Year Long Project: *http://ed.uiuc.edu/ylp*
Many science lesson ideas, including interdisciplinary lessons

Index

INDEX

INDEX

INDEX

INDEX

INDEX

INDEX